C000228479

1,000,000 Books

are available to read at

---◆---

www.ForgottenBooks.com

---◆---

Read online
Download PDF
Purchase in print

ISBN 978-0-266-05553-2
PIBN 10953933

This book is a reproduction of an important historical work. Forgotten Books uses
state-of-the-art technology to digitally reconstruct the work, preserving the original format
whilst repairing imperfections present in the aged copy. In rare cases, an imperfection in
the original, such as a blemish or missing page, may be replicated in our edition. We do,
however, repair the vast majority of imperfections successfully; any imperfections that
remain are intentionally left to preserve the state of such historical works.

1 MONTH OF
FREE
READING

at
www.ForgottenBooks.com

By purchasing this book you are eligible for one month membership to ForgottenBooks.com, giving you unlimited access to our entire collection of over 1,000,000 titles via our web site and mobile apps.

To claim your free month visit:
www.forgottenbooks.com/free953933

English
Français
Deutsche
Italiano
Español
Português

www.forgottenbooks.com

Mythology Photography **Fiction**
Fishing Christianity **Art** Cooking
Essays Buddhism Freemasonry
Medicine **Biology** Music **Ancient
Egypt** Evolution Carpentry Physics
Dance Geology **Mathematics** Fitness
Shakespeare **Folklore** Yoga Marketing
Confidence Immortality Biographies
Poetry **Psychology** Witchcraft
Electronics Chemistry History **Law**
Accounting **Philosophy** Anthropology
Alchemy Drama Quantum Mechanics
Atheism Sexual Health **Ancient History**
Entrepreneurship Languages Sport
Paleontology Needlework Islam
Metaphysics Investment Archaeology
Parenting Statistics Criminology
Motivational

Popular Government

Vol. 49/No. 2   Fall 1983

Editor: Stevens H. Clarke
Managing Editor: Margaret E. Taylor
Editorial Board: William A. Campbell, Anne M. Dellinger, Robert L. Farb, Charles D. Liner, and Warren J. Wicker
Assistant Editor: Bill Pope
Graphic Designer: C. Angela Mohr
Staff Photographer: Ted Clark

Cover Photo:
Quilting is a traditional folk art in North Carolina. Photo by C. Angela Mohr. Maps and charts by Ted Clark.

Articles

A total of 6,950 copies of this public document were printed by the Institute of Government, The University of North Carolina at Chapel Hill, at a cost of $3,611, or $.52 per copy. These figures include only the direct costs of reproduction. They do not include the preparation, handling, or distribution costs.

Managing Prosecution

Brian Forst

I t is well known that the prosecutor is a central figure in most stages of the court processing of criminal charges. The specifics, however, are less well known. Computerized data from a large number of district attorneys throughout the country reveal that about 40 per cent of all felony arrests brought to prosecutors are rejected at the screening stage or dropped soon after, usually because evidence of the crime is inadequate or because a key witness is unavailable.[1] Only 1 per cent of all felony arrests are dropped because of constitutionally inadmissible evidence.[2] Only 7

per cent of all felony arrests ever go to trial.[3] Less than one-tenth of 1 per cent are found not guilty by reason of insanity.[4] Prosecutors tend to focus on the big cases, often at the expense of many more cases that involve dangerous repeat offenders but are less interesting. Even the toughest D.A.s typically release several times as many criminal defendants as the most lenient judges release through dismissals, acquittals, and suspensions of prison sentence.

Data collected by the Institute of Government in twelve representative North Carolina counties in 1981-82 give a similar picture.[5] Of 1,193 defendants arrested and charged with felonies (serious crimes like rape, robbery, illegally enter-

ing a building to steal property, and so on), 37 per cent had all charges dismissed. In the vast majority of these cases the dismissal was made at the discretion of the prosecutor.

Prosecutors also exercise discretion by accepting pleas to lesser charges (often misdemeanors) from defendants charged with felonies. Nationwide, guilty pleas outnumber guilty verdicts by more than five to one. In the Institute's North Carolina study, 58 per cent of those charged with felonies pleaded guilty—28 per cent to a felony and 30 per cent to a misdemeanor. Thirty-nine per cent of the North Carolina defendants who pleaded guilty did so with a formal written plea bargain in which the prosecutor promised a quid pro quo (such as dismissal or reduction of some of the defendant's charges or a particular recommendation to the judge as to the sentence). Only 4 per cent of the defendants received a complete trial. The prosecutor's actions affected the sentence that defendants received, not only via charge dismissal or reduction of the charge but also directly by recommendation as to sentence; when defendants pleaded guilty to felony charges, 37 per cent of the time they did so with a formal plea bargain in which the prosecutor agreed to make a sentencing recommendation to the judge that the judge later approved.

In short, the available evidence indicates that prosecutors have a profound influence on most stages of the court processing of criminal charges, although not as often in trial or in the shadow of legal technicalities as is widely believed.

Prosecutorial decision-making

Which arrests end in conviction? Recent research in several jurisdictions shows that some factors that influence whether an arrest ends in conviction are beyond the direct control of the prosecutor: the strength of the evidence as presented to the police officer, whether crime victims and witnesses are willing to testify, the effectiveness of the officer in bringing the evidence (both tangible and testimonial) to the prosecutor, and the seriousness of the offense.[6] Other factors

The author is Director of Research at IN-SLAW, Inc., Washington, D.C. This article was adapted from *Prosecution and Sentencing, in* CRIME AND PUBLIC POLICY (Wilson ed. 1983). The author is grateful to Steve Clarke for his helpful editorial suggestions and is alone responsible for errors.

1. B. FORST, J. LUCIANOVIC, & S. COX, WHAT HAPPENS AFTER ARREST? (1977); K. BROSI, A CROSS-CITY COMPARISON OF FELONY CASE PROCESSING (1979); CALIFORNIA BUREAU OF CRIMINAL STATISTICS, ADULT FELONY ARREST DISPOSITIONS (1981).

2. B. FORST, ET AL., *id.*, at 28; K. BROSI, *id.* This is not to suggest that the practice of aborting or retarding prosecution is an appropriate response to questionable police procedures of obtaining evidence. The 10,000 or so felony cases that are rejected annually in the United States because of

such violations of due process rights may be 10,000 too many from the victims' point of view. I wish only to point out here that the problem is small from another perspective: For each case rejected because of the exclusionary rule, about 20 are rejected because the police failed to produce sufficient tangible or testimonial evidence.

3. See references at note 1 *supra.* Also, VERA INSTITUTE OF JUSTICE, FELONY ARRESTS: THEIR PROSECUTION AND DISPOSITION IN NEW YORK CITY'S COURTS (1977).

4. J. MONAHAN & H. STEADMAN, eds., MENTALLY DISORDERED OFFENDERS: PERSPECTIVES FROM LAW AND SOCIAL SCIENCES (1983).

5. See the article by Stevens H. Clarke in this issue of POPULAR GOVERNMENT.

6. B. FORST, ET AL., *op. cit. supra* note 1; B. FORST, F. LEAHY, J. SHIRHALL, H. TYSON, E.

that influence conviction are under the prosecutor's control. In determining which felony arrests brought by the police to prosecute and how vigorously to prosecute each of those that survive the arrest screening process, the district attorney must exercise some discretion. The typical urban prosecutor's office, presented with about 100 felony cases per attorney each year, obviously cannot give Watergate-level attention to every case.

For many cases the decision whether to prosecute is virtually automatic— cases in which the evidence is either extremely strong or extremely weak and cases that involve either very serious or trivial offenses. Studies have repeatedly found that the factors most closely associated with the prosecutors' decisions on case screening and handling are the strength of the evidence and the seriousness of the offense.[7] More recently, prosecutors in many jurisdictions have instituted programs to direct their efforts to cases that involve repeat offenders.[8]

Within such broad boundaries, however, prosecutors exercise a degree of decision-making latitude that has been characterized as "the greatest discretion in the formally organized criminal justice network."[9] This discretion is manifested in the D.A.s' decisions to accept cases for prosecution, to select charges to file with the court, to negotiate pleas with defense counsel, to prepare cases more or less extensively for trial, to make recommendations to the judge about bail and sentencing. Written policies used even in the most rule-conscious offices provide less than explicit instructions about how to handle each type of case. The degree of discretion that results makes it difficult

to accurately predict or clearly understand the screening, charging, and plea-bargaining decisions in particular cases.

When asked to explain the rationale behind their decisions, most prosecutors are inclined to say that case-handling decisions, like medical decisions, involve both science and craft, and that experienced prosecutors know how to blend the technical requirements of the law with the good judgment that comes from years of practice. This tells us nothing, however, about the underlying goals that influence the decision-making process and nothing about whether the prosecutor consciously makes decisions on the selection and handling of cases with such goals in mind. While prosecutors say that their goals include justice, crime control, and speedy processing, they consider each case as unique. Many prosecutors believe that decisions about whether to accept a case, what charges to file, how much time to spend preparing the case for a court proceeding, or what charge or charges to allow the defendant to plead to in return for the dropping of other charges (or what sentence to recommend to the judge if the defendant pleads guilty to a particular charge) need to be made on a case-by-case basis, rather than by pondering over abstract goals or resorting to a formula that derives from such goals.[10]

"Career criminal" programs

A shift toward a more structured approach to exercising discretion occurred in 1975 with the initiation of the Law Enforcement Assistance Administration's (LEAA) "career criminal" prosecution program. This program was designed to deal with the problem posed by a relatively few offenders who, researchers were beginning to find, accounted for a disproportionate share of cases involving serious crimes.[11] It had been perceived

generally that prosecutors did not give extra attention to cases involving these more criminally active offenders, cases that were often otherwise unattractive (e.g., because the offense was not very serious or because a key witness was reluctant to testify). This perception was later confirmed by empirical study.[12] To provide an incentive for prosecutors to allocate more time to such cases, LEAA offered grants to local prosecutors for the creation of career criminal programs. Many prosecutors, interested in the additional resources, applied for and obtained them.

Subsequent evaluations of those programs have indicated that career criminal units have indeed allocated more resources to their cases than are applied to conventionally processed cases—perhaps four or five times more.[13] The evidence suggests, however, that the criteria used by career criminal units to select cases, while they have contributed to a more structured exercise of discretion, have not been carefully geared to identify the most dangerous offenders and thus reduce crime—the point of the program and, presumably, a fundamental goal of criminal prosecution. The criteria, instead, have been established in most jurisdictions to be simple and safe to administer and to produce cases that interest career criminal attorneys. Career criminal units have typically targeted on offenders with at least one prior felony conviction and current charges involving a serious crime— often homicide, rape, or assault. While those criteria are better than none, for purposes of crime control, prosecutors can do much better.

More consistent with the idea of reducing crime by convicting and incarcerating the most dangerous and criminally active offenders would be the

Wish. & J. Bartolomeo, Arrest Convictability As a Measure of Police Performance (1981).

7. Forst & Brosi. *A Theoretical and Empirical Analysis of the Prosecutor.* 6 J. Legal Stud. 177-91 (1977); U.S. Department of Justice, Justice Litigation Management (1977); J. Jacoby, Prosecutorial Decisionmaking: A National Study (1981).

8. E. Chelimsky & J. Dahmann, Career Criminal Program National Evaluation; Final Report (1981); Chelimsky & Dahmann, *The MITRE Corporation's National Evaluation of the Career Criminal Program: A Discussion of the Findings.* 71 J. Crim. Law & Criminology 102-06 (1980).

9. A. Reiss. *Discretionary Justice in the United States.* 2 Int'l J. Criminology & Penology (1974).

10. A. Gelman. Report of a Survey of U.S. Attorneys and Federal Investigative Agents (1981).

11. In 1972, Marvin Wolfgang and his associates at the University of Pennsylvania reported that 18 per cent of a group of juvenile delinquents in Philadelphia accounted for 52 per cent of all the offenses committed by the group. M. Wolfgang, R. Figlio. & T. Sellin. Delinquency in Birth Cohort 88 (1972). Then in 1976 Kristen Williams, analyzing PROMIS data from

the District of Columbia for 1971-75, found that 7 per cent of the 46,000 different defendants arrested accounted for 24 per cent of the 73,000 felony and serious misdemeanor cases handled by the prosecutor for that jurisdiction. Those findings appeared in a 1976 working paper by Williams and in a finished version in 1979—The Scope and Prediction of Recidivism 5-6 (1979).

12. See note 7 and accompanying text.

13. E. Chelimsky & J. Dahmann, op. cit. *supra* note 8. It has been found that separate career criminal units within prosecutors' offices may actually allocate excessive resources to cases involving repeat offenders. Rhodes. *Investment of Prosecution Resources in Career Criminal Cases.* 71 J. Crim. Law & Criminology 118-23 (1980).

use of criteria that correspond more closely to what is widely known about the characteristics of those offenders: prior arrests for serious crime, a juvenile record, youthfulness, drug use, and known involvement in robbery or burglary. These characteristics have been established empirically by researchers at the University of Pennsylvania, the Rand Corporation, and INSLAW as the strongest known predictors of predatory crime; yet they have been omitted, for the most part, from criteria for targeting career criminals.[14] The public has been deeply concerned about crime, but the implications of widespread use of targeting criteria that focus largely on career offenders near the end of their careers, without really removing the offenders who inflict the most harm on society, appear to have escaped public scrutiny. The career criminal program thus stands to be improved; more fundamentally, however, the fact that D.A.s have accepted the basic concept of the program in the first place represents a significant departure from the conventional approach to prosecution.

Modern management technology

Many prosecutors have recently begun to depart from the traditional prosecution practices in other ways as well to achieve greater accountability, uniformity, and efficiency in the decisions and practices that follow arrest. In the 1970s many prosecutors throughout the country began to use computerized information-processing systems for tracking individual cases and caseloads of individual attorneys, printing subpoenas, producing periodic reports that show various dimensions of office performance in the aggregate, and providing data so that office

policy could be analyzed in depth.[15] The proliferation of these systems indicates that prosecutors experience benefits from them that exceed the costs. And despite the limitations of career criminal programs noted above, the fact that these programs have been retained after federal support was withdrawn shows that prosecutors have become increasingly aware of the need to manage their offices to accomplish goals as broad as crime control.

Perhaps the most significant aspect of these reforms is that they were initiated with the full involvement of the prosecutor. Other attempts to reform prosecution practices have been less successful. For example, efforts to abolish plea bargaining that have not had the full support of the prosecutor have been circumvented—sentence bargaining has replaced charge bargaining, and the rate at which prosecutors have dropped cases has increased.[16]

Further reform

Until recently, prosecutors have operated in a statistical darkness that is uncharacteristic of other components of the criminal justice system and inconsistent with contemporary standards of management and public accountability. The statistical information that is now beginning to accumulate in several jurisdictions represents a fundamental reform of prosecution. This information should help district attorneys to augment their single-case litigation perspective, instilled by conventional legal training, with one that considers the aggregate information in the context of goals of prosecution.

Prosecution can advance further with the refinement of guidelines for decision-making by prosecutors and with the further production, dissemination, and use of sound statistical information to support those decisions. The process of developing these guidelines is itself important for its tendency to induce more systematic

consideration of the goals of justice and how to achieve them. Once developed, the guidelines can serve as explicit statements of policy to foster more consistent and effective decision-making by prosecutors. The box on the next page shows how such guidelines are being used in Mecklenburg County.

Prosecution guidelines also provide standards against which the D.A. can use data to assess the performance of his office. If the data indicate that the guideline standards are consistently too high—for example, overly stringent screening standards may produce too many voluntary dismissals—a conscious choice can then be made either to relax the guidelines or to improve performance.[17]

The computerized prosecution data that are now being produced in many states (unfortunately, North Carolina is not yet one) can also be used to assess and improve the prosecutor's criteria for (1) screening out cases and selecting charges to file in court for the rest, (2) identifying cases that merit extra effort to obtain convictions, and (3) making recommendations to the judge on bail and sentence. Recent research shows that criteria derived from empirical analysis of large computerized data bases maintained by prosecutors and courts can yield results that substantially surpass those associated with criteria ordinarily used at each of these important stages of decision-making.

A useful example is provided by the prosecutor's bail recommendations. Many of those arrested on felony charges who are detained in jail pending trial have been found to have characteristics that make them predictably less prone to pretrial misconduct than others who are released. By basing their pretrial release and detention recommendations on the defendant's rating, derived from these characteristics, prosecutors could conceivably induce judges to reduce jail populations substantially with no increases in either pretrial crime or failures to appear in court.[18]

14. M. WOLFGANG, ET AL., op. cit. supra note 11; K. WILLIAMS, op. cit. supra note 11; B. FORST, W. RHODES, J. DIMM, A. GELMAN, AND B. MULLIN, TARGETING FEDERAL RESOURCES ON RECIDIVISTS (1982); P. GREENWOOD, SELECTIVE INCAPACITATION (1982); J. CHAIKEN & M. CHAIKEN, VARIETIES OF CRIMINAL BEHAVIOR (1982).

For a comparison of the effects of empirically derived identification criteria with conventional (LEAA-recommended) criteria on crime control, see Williams, Selection Criteria for Career Criminal Programs, 71 J. CRIM. LAW & CRIMINOLOGY 89-93 (1980).

15. The nation's most widely used automated record-keeping system for prosecutors, PROMIS, was first installed in the U.S. Attorney's Office for Washington, D.C., under federal funding in 1970. It is now used in approximately 100 jurisdictions, including several federal districts.

16. A. BLUMSTEIN, ET AL., eds., RESEARCH ON SENTENCING: THE SEARCH FOR REFORM (1983).

17. This might be done through improving evidence, using investigative resources available to the prosecutor more efficiently, or increasing witness support by maintaining better contact with witnesses, perhaps by means of paralegal assistants.

18. Jeffrey Roth and Paul Wice have estimated, specifically, that by incorporating factors that have been found not to be used in the bail decision—such as involvement in illegal drugs—and discarding factors that have been used in the bail deci-

An essential element in improving each of the major prosecution decisions—from screening to sentence recommendations—is reliable data about each of the elements that are germane to those decisions. Prosecutors are usually quick to express concern, as they should, about the need for prompt, reliable information from investigators, forensic laboratories, and lineups. If that information adds up to a convictable case, a well-managed prosecution system oriented toward crime control would also collect data on the defendant's dangerousness, including his arrest history ("rap sheet"), whether he has a serious juvenile record, and whether he is a drug user. Prosecutors and judges have not been conditioned to seek such information to support decisions on prosecution and sentencing despite widespread concern about "false positives"—people selected for extra prosecution effort and eventual incarceration who in fact would not commit another crime if released. The availability and use of reliable rap sheets, juvenile records, and information about drug abuse, when combined with existing information, would provide demonstrably more accurate assessments of dangerousness than current information alone can provide; more accurate assessment means *fewer* false positives.[19]

Data used by prosecutors and courts, properly processed, can also be disseminated usefully outside the offices that pro-

(continued on page 10)

sion but have not been found to be related to pretrial misconduct—such as whether the defendant has a local residence—jail populations could be reduced by about 20 per cent with no increase in the rate of failure to appear, or by about 40 per cent with no increase in the pretrial rearrest rate. J. ROTH & P. WICE, PRETRIAL RELEASE AND MISCONDUCT IN THE DISTRICT OF COLUMBIA (1980).

19. It is occasionally argued that statistical prediction should not be used as a basis for decision-making in the field of criminal justice because of the false-positives problem. In truth, nonstatistical assessment of dangerousness—the method preferred in most jurisdictions—has repeatedly been found to produce false positives at a *higher* rate than statistical assessments. See, for example, P. MEEHL, CLINICAL VS. STATISTICAL PREDICTION (1954); Steadman & Cocozza, *Psychiatry, Dangerousness and the Repetitively Violent Offender*, 69 J. CRIM. LAW & CRIMINOLOGY 226-31 (1978); J. MONAHAN, PREDICTING VIOLENT BEHAVIOR: AN ASSESSMENT OF CLINICAL TECHNIQUES (1981); and J. Carroll, et al., *Evaluation, Diagnosis, and Prediction in Parole Decision Making*, 17 LAW & SOCIETY REV. 199-228 (1982).

New Breed: The Management-Conscious District Attorney

One of the modern prosecutors referred to in the accompanying article is Peter Gilchrist, District Attorney for Mecklenburg County (Charlotte), North Carolina. A seasoned prosecutor (Charlotte's D.A. since 1975), Gilchrist is also a prominent member of the new class of management-conscious district attorneys.

State funds have not yet been available to support Gilchrist's plans for an automated management information system. In the meantime, he has put to use in his office a number of other management tools available to the prosecutor of the 1980s.

A centerpiece of Gilchrist's prosecution system is his use of empirically derived criteria for identifying career criminals. Arrests that are accepted as cases by any of Gilchrist's assistant district attorneys and filed in the Mecklenburg County Court fall into four categories: conventional felony prosecution, misdemeanor prosecution, diversion to a rehabilitation program, and career criminal prosecution.

The defendant who scores 55 on Gilchrist's career criminal guidelines system qualifies as a "career criminal." Defendants accumulate points to the extent that they correspond to the statistical profile of the high crime rate, dangerous offender—one who has a recent criminal record (for example, four points for each arrest for a violent crime within the past five years, 45 points for a prior prison term of more than four years); who is a heroin user (10 points) or a heavy alcohol user (5 points); who is young; and whose current offense involves robbery, breaking and entering, or another crime commonly committed by the active street offender. While these characteristics have not yet been validated specifically for Mecklenburg County, they have been found in jurisdiction after jurisdiction to be predictive of later predatory crime.

Why the new system? According to Gilchrist: "The ever-increasing number of defendants brought to our court requires that we prosecutors develop sound methods to identify both the people and the crimes that we must invest our available resources in. We feel that the use of scientifically valid criteria can best identify for our office the 5 to 6 per cent of the defendants who are the most criminally active in Mecklenburg County."

Prosecuting cases involving dangerous offenders is not always easy, and Gilchrist is willing to give them special attention not ordinarily given to other cases: "Our biggest problem with the cases involving these identified defendants is the failure of the civilian witnesses who are necessary for successful prosecution to appear in court. Frequently, the witnesses in these cases fail to respond to ordinary subpoenas, and the cases are lost due to their absence in court. To solve this problem we have directed an investigator to contact the witnesses for these cases prior to court, to attempt to ensure their attendance."

Gilchrist's strategy is consistent with the empirical evidence. Research on both police and prosecution has consistently revealed the central importance of witness support to successful prosecution. Keeping witnesses assured and informed takes some time but can have a big payoff in getting offenders convicted. When the offenders are dangerous, these convictions are bound to help control crime.—BF

The Public Defender Program in North Carolina

Frederick G. Lind

From the first, let me acknowledge that I am a partisan of the public defender system. My nine years of experience with the system and professional and scholarly studies both convince me that it is the best way to provide legal counsel to indigents who are charged with criminal offenses. This article will describe the public defender system in North Carolina, show how the system works in practice, and then examine some arguments for and against it.

Indigents' right to representation in criminal cases was established in two landmark cases before the United States Supreme Court. In *Gideon v. Wainwright* (1963)[1] the Court held that states must furnish free legal representation for an indigent charged with a felony, and in *Argersinger v. Hamlin* (1972)[2] it held that an indigent could not be sentenced to prison unless he or she either had free counsel appointed or had knowingly, voluntarily, and intelligently waived counsel. North Carolina law [G.S. 7A-451(a)(1)] conforms to these requirements by giving indigents the right to appointed counsel in "(a)ny

case in which imprisonment, or a fine of five hundred dollars ($500), or more is likely to be adjudged" and in hearings for revocation of probation, extradition hearings, involuntary commitment proceedings, juvenile hearings, and hearings on a petition for a writ of habeas corpus under G.S. Chapter 17.

The Supreme Court has left the definition of "indigent" up to the states. North Carolina law [G.S. 7A-450(a)] defines an indigent as a "person who is financially unable to secure legal representation and to provide all other necessary expenses of representation in an action or proceeding enumerated in the Subchapter."

Seven of the state's thirty-four judicial districts meet their obligation to indigents by maintaining an office of public defender. (The seven judicial districts include twelve counties.) In the other twenty-seven, the court assigns private lawyers to represent indigent clients. The method of this assignment is supposed to be governed by rules drawn up by the North Carolina State Bar Council,[3] but the North Carolina Courts Commission reports that the method of assignment is

usually determined by the senior regular resident superior court judge and not by the district bar, as the law contemplates.[4] When the lawyer has finished representing an indigent, a judge determines the appropriate fee, which Administrative Office of the Courts (AOC) pays from a special indigency fund.[5]

indigency, the waiver of counsel, the adoption and approval of plans by any district bar regarding the method of assignment of counsel among the licensed attorneys of the district, and such other matters as shall provide for the protection of the constitutional rights of all indigent persons and the reasonable allocation of responsibility for the representation of indigent persons among the licensed attorneys of the State."

4. N.C. GEN. STAT. § 7A-459; NORTH CAROLINA COURTS COMMISSION, SUPPLEMENTAL REPORT TO THE 1983 GENERAL ASSEMBLY (April 6, 1983).

5. N.C. GEN. STAT. § G.S. 7A-458 prescribes how the fee is to be determined: "[I]n districts which do not have a public defender, the court shall fix the fee to which an attorney who represents an indigent person is entitled. In doing so, the court shall allow a fee based on the factors normally considered in fixing attorney's fees usually charged in similar cases. Fees shall be fixed by the district court judge for actions or proceedings finally determined in the district court and by the superior court judge for actions or proceedings originating in, heard on appeal in, or appealed from the superior court. Even if the trial, appeal, hearing or other proceeding is never held, preparation therefor is nevertheless compensable."

The author is assistant public defender in the Eighteenth Judicial District (Guilford County).

1. 372 U.S. 335, 83 S.Ct. 792, 9 L.Ed. 2d 799 (1963).

2. 407 U.S. 25, 92 S.Ct. 2006, 32 L.Ed. 2d 530 (1972).

3. N.C. GEN. STAT. § 7A-459 reads as follows: "The North Carolina State Bar Council shall make rules and regulations consistent with this article relating to the manner and method of assigning counsel, the procedure for the determination of

The law provides some methods for the state to recoup the costs of defending indigent criminal defendants—although according to the latest study by the AOC,[6] only about 10 per cent of the costs are in fact recovered. When an indigent defendant has been represented by the public defender or assigned counsel, the judge must assign an attorney cost to the case.[7] This cost will be either the fee paid to the private lawyer who is appointed or the fee that is set for record-keeping purposes as the value of the public defender services. It is recorded as a judgment debt in the clerk of court's office, but the defendant will not necessarily pay for it.[8]

A second method of recouping counsel costs is for the trial court to make a condition of a suspended prison sentence that the defendant pay for the legal fee incurred as a result of the appointment of a lawyer. But this suspended prison sentence cannot be activated if the probationer can show that he, in good faith, cannot pay.[9]

Figure 1

Judicial Districts with Public Defender Offices

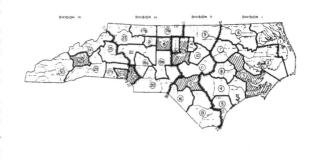

The public defender system began in North Carolina on January 1, 1970, when defenders' offices were established in the 18th (Guilford County) and 12th (Cumberland and Hoke counties) judicial districts. As Figure 1 shows, the system has expanded over the

6. NORTH CAROLINA COURTS COMMISSION, op. cit. supra, note 4, p. 1.

7. N.C. GEN. STAT. § 7A-455(b).

8. The North Carolina Supreme Court has held that, despite the requirement of N.C. Gen. Stat. § 7A-455(b) that the counsel cost be directly recorded as a judgment debt, the debt is invalid unless the defendant has received notice and a hearing and the trial court has made findings of fact and conclusions of law to justify the debt, pursuant to Rule 52 of the Rules of Civil Procedure. State v. Crews, 284 N.C. 427, 201 S.E.2d 840 (1974). Also, the indigent defendant who is unable to pay counsel costs after his case is disposed of could presumably invoke the statutory insolvent debtor's procedure and discharge the debt. N.C. GEN. STAT. Ch. 23, Art. 4.

9. State v. Young, 21 N.C. App. 316 (1974); cf. N.C. GEN. STAT. § 15A-1361 et seq. on non-payment of fines; on an equal protection point, see also Fuller v. Oregon, 417 U.S. 40 (1974), which upheld an Oregon scheme allowing probationer to show that he was unable to pay as defense to revocation for failure to pay assigned counsel costs.

last fourteen years. Public defender offices have been established in judicial districts 28 (Buncombe, 1973), 26 (Mecklenburg, 1975), 27 (Gaston, Lincoln, and Cleveland, 1975), 27A (Gaston County, 1978), 3 (Pitt, Craven, Pamlico, and Carteret, 1981), and 15B (Chatham and Orange, 1983).

Public defenders are appointed by the Governor (except in the 28th judicial district, where he is appointed by the senior resident superior court judge of that district) from a list of not less than two and not more than three names nominated by written ballot of the attorneys resident in the district who are licensed to practice law in North Carolina. The balloting is to be conducted pursuant to regulations promulgated by the AOC.[10] Defenders' terms of office are for four years, beginning on the dates specified in that section for each district.[11]

In the judicial districts where the public defender has not been established, the courts use the assigned-counsel system so that the two systems for representing indigents work side by side. In both systems, the court must find a person in-

10. N.C. GEN. STAT. § 7A-466.

11. Id. § 7A-465.

digent in order for a lawyer to be appointed. If the defendant is charged with a criminal offense, the judge usually appoints counsel in either the district or superior court. The defendant will fill out an affidavit of indigency by which the court can determine how much money and property he owns and what debts are owed to or by him. On the basis of this application and perhaps some oral questioning of the defendant, the judge either finds that he is indigent and appoints counsel or denies appointment on grounds that he can afford to pay for his own lawyer. If appointed counsel is denied, the judge usually allows a continuance for the defendant to employ a lawyer.

In public defender districts, most indigents are represented by the public defender's office. But sometimes there may be a conflict of interest, and a private lawyer from that district will be appointed to represent the person whom the public defender cannot ethically represent—for example, when there are two indigent co-defendants and one has incriminated the other.[12] The appointment of private

12. This incriminating statement made by one defendant would make this defendant a potential State's witness to be used against one or more other

counsel in such a conflict is often from a list of private practitioners who will accept appointment in indigent cases. Often the judge appoints private counsel in the order their names appear on a list to achieve a somewhat systematic and equitable approach to appointment of private counsel in indigent cases. The AOC estimates that at least 10 per cent of the indigent cases in a public defender district must be handled by assigned private counsel to avoid conflicts of interest.[13]

Since 1980 the Office of the Appellate Defender has existed along with the public defenders. This office operates on a statewide basis and specializes in appeals of indigents. It has a staff of seven lawyers, including two who primarily handle capital cases and two who handle cases in the Court of Appeals. The office handles approximately 140 appeals each year.

P ublic defender offices primarily handle criminal cases—traffic, larceny, breaking or entering, assault, arson, robbery, sexual offenses, rape, and murder. Generally the representation is "vertical," in that one lawyer stays with the case through all levels of representation. For example, if the public defender is to represent a defendant on a murder case, a lawyer on the staff will handle the probable cause hearing in district court and will stay with the case through the superior court proceedings, at which there will be either a guilty or no-contest plea and sentence by the judge or a not-guilty plea and a jury trial. If the jury finds the defendant guilty, he has a right to appeal. The same lawyer may han-

defendants. It would be unethical for a lawyer in the public defender's office to represent the person who makes the incriminating statement and also those who are incriminated by the statement. Often, when two or more defendants are charged with the same crime, a judge will see a potential conflict of interest and appoint the public defender to represent one defendant and appoint separate lawyers from the private bar to represent the other defendants.

13. R. E. GILES, COMPARATIVE COST ESTIMATES FOR ESTABLISHING ADDITIONAL PUBLIC DEFENDER OFFICES IN CERTAIN JUDICIAL DISTRICTS (Raleigh, N.C.: N.C. Administrative Office of the Courts, June 13, 1983).

dle the appeal, or the Appellate Defender may be appointed to handle it.

The Guilford County Public Defender Office is one of the two original offices. Guilford County is the only one that has two seats of superior court—in High Point and in Greensboro. There are nine staff lawyers in Greensboro and three in High Point. All but two of these lawyers handle predominantly felony cases, with an occasional misdemeanor case. The Guilford County office handles approximately 3,000 cases per year, and its legal staff averages about five years of public defender experience.

District 12 includes Cumberland and Hoke counties. The nine lawyers in the public defender office (in Fayetteville) average about three and a half years of public defender experience. They handle approximately 2,400 cases per year. Three of the lawyers handle mostly misdemeanor cases and the remaining six mostly felonies. One of these six handles all of the cases out of Hoke County for six months.

District 26 comprises Mecklenburg County. The public defender's office in Charlotte has fifteen lawyers, who handle about 5,000 cases a year. Half of the legal staff predominantly handle misdemeanors and the rest mostly handle felonies.

District 28 (Buncombe County) has a public defender office with four lawyers and an annual caseload of approximately 1,600. Three of the four lawyers handle both misdemeanors and felonies, and the fourth handles judicial hospitalizations and juvenile cases. The staff averages approximately six years of public defender experience.

District 27A has a public defender office in Gastonia. The annual caseload is about 1,600. There are five lawyers on the staff, all of whom handle both misdemeanors and felonies. Two of the staff also handle some juvenile cases. The office does not handle judicial hospitalization cases.

District 3 includes Pitt, Craven, Pamlico, and Carteret counties. It handles approximately 1,400 cases, two-thirds of them coming from Pitt County. The main public defender office for this district is in Greenville. That office has four lawyers who handle both misdemeanors and felonies, one of whom specializes in serious felonies. In a New Bern branch office, two lawyers handle all of the indigent cases in Craven and Pamlico counties. One lawyer staffs the Beaufort branch office and handles all Cartaret County cases.

The new public defender office for District 15B (Orange and Chatham counties) has two lawyers.

L et's follow a typical breaking or entering case that goes to a jury trial in Guilford County. Sam Jackson is the defendant. First, the public defender (PD) gets a file from the court clerk's office containing the warrant that charges Sam with felonious breaking or entering and larceny. He reads the warrant and sees that Sam is alleged to have broken into the Florida Street Curb Market, located on Florida Street in Greensboro, and stolen four cases of beer and approximately $150 in cash. The warrant lists as witnesses only the owner of the curb market and Detective Randolph of the Greensboro Police Department. The file indicates that Sam is in jail under a $2,000 secured bond.

The PD goes to talk to Sam. He tells Sam that anything Sam says to him about the case will be confidential and the PD will not reveal it to anyone unless he thinks that it will benefit Sam. The PD also tells Sam not to say anything about the case to anybody—if a police officer or any other law enforcement officers want to talk to him, he should tell them to see his lawyer. The PD gets a lot of background information from Sam, including the fact that he already has a conviction for breaking or entering and larceny. Sam tells PD that although he has a record, he was in no way involved in the curb market break-in. He says that on the date of the break-in he worked at a local restaurant all day and was at home with his parents that evening. Sam says that if his bond is lowered to $500, his family might be able to raise the $75 needed to get a bondsman to secure his release.

PD returns to his office, calls Detective Randolph, and asks him about the charge against Sam. Randolph says that one of his informants put him onto Joey Banks as a suspect in this break-in. Banks, after being advised of his rights, made a statement to Randolph that he and his brother Luther met up with Sam on Friday evening. The three decided to break into the curb market. Banks said that he broke out a window and opened it, and he and his brother went in while Sam stood outside as lookout. Then he and his brother handed out four cases of beer to Sam and they all left. Banks claimed that

Sam got a case of beer and $50 of the $150 that Banks took out of the cash register.

PD asks Randolph what he thinks about a bail bond reduction for Sam. Randolph says that he thinks that Sam should have secured bond, but he has no objection to the amount being lowered to $1,000 or $500.

PD calls Tom Williams, the assistant district attorney, who is in charge of handling felony cases in district court. Williams knows nothing about the case, so PD tells him that Sam is charged with a break-in but perhaps the main evidence against him will be testimony from an accomplice. PD tells Williams that Sam has some record, but he is from Guilford County and lives with his family and is working and likely will return to court. He also tells Williams that he is asking for a bond hearing on that Friday.

PD prepares a request for a bond hearing for the clerk of court and for the police liaison officer, Larry James. This request tells the defendant's name, the court date, the date on which the bond hearing is requested, and the names of the police officers on the case. PD talks to the assistant district attorney, who says that he will recommend a $500 bond to the court. PD says that he will ask the judge to release Sam into his parents' custody so that he will save a bond premium.

PD calls the restaurant to verify that Sam works there and learns that he has been a good employee for six months. PD arranges with Sam's father to be in court about 10 o'clock on Friday morning.

PD asks his investigator to check for any criminal record on Sam and also for any record on the Banks brothers. He also asks the investigator to find anyone who will testify that either or both of the Banks brothers have a bad reputation in their community. If this evidence is available, PD could use it to impeach the Banks boys' testimony.

At the bond hearing PD asks the bailiffs to bring Sam into the courtroom. He also makes sure that Williams, the assistant district attorney, either will be in the courtroom or has relayed his bond recommendation to whichever prosecutor will be in the district court. Williams appears himself and tells the judge that he would not oppose a secured bond of $1,000. PD tells the court of Sam's job and good work record and points out that Sam's father is in the courtroom, and he asks that Sam either be released into his parents' custody or allowed to sign an unsecured bond. The court reduces the bond amount to $500. Sam posts the bond and is released from jail.

Sam returns to district court for his probable cause hearing. He has been out of jail for several weeks and is doing well. The assistant district attorney, Williams, says that he will not reduce Sam's case to a misdemeanor even if Sam pleads guilty. Williams asks PD to "waive the case up" to superior court—i.e., to forego Sam's right to a probable cause hearing. PD says that he will be willing to waive the hearing if he can get a copy of Joey Banks's statement (knowing that this is not a document that he can legally compel Williams to provide). Williams says that he will not give him a copy but will let PD read Banks's statement. PD agrees and reads the statement, making mental notes of those parts that implicate Sam. The statement is not very detailed.

Within a few days after waiving Sam's probable cause hearing, PD files a written request for "discovery," which will entitle him to find out some of the state's evidence. Several weeks later the grand jury indicts Sam, and the case is placed on the superior court docket. PD has Sam sign a written waiver of his right to arraignment, which PD files, so that Sam need not take several hours off from work just to say that he pleads not guilty. PD also examines a copy of the indictment to see whether it contains any legal flaws.[14] PD feels that the indictment is adequate but believes that Sam would have a good chance by going to trial.

PD talks with the prosecutor to see what he can find out about the evidence against Sam. He learns that the offense allegedly occurred about midnight, which is when Banks's statement claimed it occurred. PD learns that the evidence room in the police department has three cases of beer taken from Banks that supposedly came from the curb market.

PD goes to the evidence room to see the beer. Nothing appears unusual. PD notes mentally that no mention has been made of fingerprints. He concludes that

since DA has said nothing about fingerprints, he must not have any. PD realizes that in his closing argument to the jury he can point out that if what Banks says about handing the beer to Sam is true, Sam's fingerprints would be all over the beer cans, and there is absolutely no corroboration to Banks's testimony.

PD has learned that Banks has a bad record—has several convictions and has had other charges dismissed. PD looked through the court files on every local case ever brought that involved Banks. Even a case that has been dismissed is useful, because PD can ask Banks whether he committed the offense charged if there is a good-faith basis to believe—despite the dismissal—that Banks did commit it. PD gets copies of most of these files on Banks's record.

PD has conferred with Sam every two weeks since Sam got out of jail. PD and Sam decide that it will be better not to put Sam on the witness stand, in light of the apparent weakness of the state's case, so that his criminal record cannot be revealed in cross-examination. (If Sam did testify, the State could ask about his prior convictions.) Sam's family are prepared to testify that he was at home the night of the break-in.

PD files subpoenas for all the members of Sam's family whom he wants to testify and tells them that they need to report to the clerk's office so that they will get their $5/day witness fee.

PD prepares his opening statement, cross-examination of Banks, direct examination of the family, closing argument, and other strategy before trial. He also prepares written instructions that he will request from the judge.

The trial begins, and the jury is selected. PD delivers a carefully prepared opening statement that tells the jury to note both Banks's bad record and the State's promise to him that in exchange for his testimony he will not receive an active prison sentence.

In testimony Banks makes a bad witness. The State's case is weak. At recess DA offers to let Sam plead guilty to a misdemeanor and get probation, but Sam says he is not guilty and wants to complete the trial. His family testifies. While they are not very articulate, they show much concern for Sam.

Closing arguments are delivered and PD hammers away at Banks's unreliability. The judge instructs the jury as PD had requested. From here on, Sam's fate is up to the jury.

---

14. If perhaps the indictment does not contain certain allegations, it may not give jurisdiction for the case to be tried in superior court. In that event the district attorney might not notice the flaw; if the case were tried, it would be a "free" trial for Sam in that if he were found not guilty, that would be the end of the case. If he were convicted, however, the public defender could raise the fact that the court had no jurisdiction and get the conviction set aside.

A s I said earlier, I believe in the public defender system, having spent nearly nine years as an assistant public defender. Aside from this subjective judgment, however, there are several arguments to be made for expanding the system.

The main advantage of the public defender system is that it represents indigent defendants effectively and efficiently. The public defender lawyer *specializes* in handling criminal cases. G.S 7A-465 provides that the public defender "shall devote his full time to the duties of his office." The lawyer on a public defender staff becomes expert in defending those charged with a criminal offense, just as another lawyer may become expert in tax or estate work.

The public defender's specialization is important in that he is constantly available to the courts, and cases are therefore disposed in court much faster than they otherwise would be. For example, a lawyer with the public defender's office will not be handling a case in another county or in federal court or in a civil court when the DA wants to call his case for trial. Public defender offices are either in or very near the courthouse, so that the defender can work in his office while waiting for his case to come to trial, whereas a privately appointed lawyer would have to sit in the courtroom for several hours waiting for a case to be called (and would no doubt ask compensation for his "sitting time").

Another important feature of the public defender system is that each office is provided with at least one full-time investigator and one full-time secretary, which furthers effective representation.

The fact that all members on the public defender's staff are involved in criminal defense work allows them to talk together about their cases to try to develop productive new ways of representing clients.

Furthermore, the public defender office is a service to both lawyers who are assigned an indigent case and other lawyers who are handling private cases. These lawyers come to the public defender office to seek advice, copies of motions, and any other information related to complex or seldom-litigated legal matters that are routine for the public defender. Local lawyers appreciate the criminal defense materials that the public defender can provide.

Recent studies indicate that public defenders represent their clients more ef-

> *The main advantage of the public defender system is that it represents indigents effectively and efficiently . . . the public defender specializes in handling criminal cases.*

fectively than assigned private lawyers, as the North Carolina Bar Association Foundation's *Final Report* (1976) of the Special Committee on Indigent Legal Services Delivery Systems (hereafter NCBA Report) shows. The committee sent questionnaires to all district and superior court judges in the state, of whom about 70 per cent responded. The judges rated the public defenders twice as likely as assigned attorneys in felony cases to have first contact with their clients within one day of arrest and over three times as likely to have contact within the first day in a misdemeanor case. Moreover, 42 per cent of the judges characterized the defender's professional reputation within the legal community as "excellent" and 47 per cent characterized it as "good." Also, 38 per cent of the judges rated the defender's representation of indigents "excellent" and 53 per cent rated it "good." In contrast, only 19 per cent of the judges rated assigned private counsel "excellent" and 66 per cent rated it "good."

Furthermore, a comparison in the NCBA Report of indigent defendant cases represented by public defenders and by assigned private lawyers shows that clients of public defenders significantly less often plead guilty to the original charge and more often plead guilty to a lesser offense.[15]

Similarly, an Institute of Government study[16] found that felony defendants, whether charged with violent felonies or theft felonies like breaking or entering, were more likely to have their charges dismissed when represented by the public defender than when represented by assigned private counsel, other things being

equal. The likelihood of dismissal was about the same for defendants with privately paid counsel and defendants represented by the public defender.

Another important advantage of the public defender system is its low cost. While cost should not be a pre-eminent consideration in defending those who cannot pay for their own legal fees, it is certainly important to the legislature and the taxpayer. It is worth noting that the privately assigned system will exceed its budgeted funds by an estimated $3.1 million in 1983-84.[17] The North Carolina Courts Commission recommended that the General Assembly consider establishing a public defender's office in additional districts where it would be cost effective to do so.[18] This recommendation was largely based on a report done by the State Budget Office at the Commission's request. The report concluded, on the basis of an evaluation of data from the 1980-81 fiscal year, that the average cost per case for public defenders is significantly lower than for assigned counsel—$130, compared with $186.[19]

The AOC, at the Commission's request, studied the costs of representing indigent defendants. It concluded that unless a district is spending at least $225,000 per year for assigned counsel, the public defender system will not save money. The AOC study indicated that the public defender system would bring net savings in districts 4, 7, 5, 8, 10, and 14 (including Durham, Raleigh, Wilmington, and some other urban areas) totaling an estimated $352,000 per year.[20]

One objection to the public defender system has been that it denies young lawyers in the local bar the experience

15. NORTH CAROLINA BAR ASSOCIATION FOUNDATION, SPECIAL COMMITTEE ON INDIGENT LEGAL SERVICES DELIVERY SYSTEMS, FINAL REPORT, 82-83 (Raleigh, N.C.: North Carolina Bar Association, 1976).

16. S. CLARKE, S. KURTZ, E. RUBINSKY, & D. SCHLEICHER, FELONY PROSECUTION AND SENTENCING IN NORTH CAROLINA 39-40, Tables 11, 12 (Institute of Government 1982).

17. *Op. cit. supra* note 4, at 1-2. The Courts Commission is working on alleviating this financial crisis, which seems to have arisen from an increased caseload rather than mismanagement of the program.

18. *Op. cit. supra* note 4.

19. *Id.*

20. GILES, *op. cit. supra* note 13, at 9-10.

they need to develop into able trial lawyers. The Courts Commission addressed this point in its recent report to the General Assembly:

> The Commission believes it is desirable to have as many private lawyers as possible actively participating in the criminal courts, for many reasons, and to that end it recommends that any public defender's office be staffed and expected to handle no more than 70 per cent of the indigent defense work in the district. Cases in which the public defender's office cannot ethically represent a defendant will always require some assigned counsel to be used, but the Commission believes the State's policy should go beyond that minimum.[21]

Such a policy may be a way to provide experience to young lawyers. But young lawyers hired as assistant public defenders get experience too. In fact, they probably learn criminal defense work much faster and better than they would if they got occasional assignments to defend indigents. Also, because young assistant public defenders are supervised by an experienced specialist (the public defender), the client may be less likely to suffer from mistakes of inexperience than if he were represented by young assigned counsel. In any event, there is a serious question as to the propriety of sacrificing the indigent defendant as a "guinea pig" for the development of the fledgling (assigned) lawyer.

Another objection to the public defender system is that the defenders are paid by the state, just as the prosecutors are, and may therefore be too cooperative with the prosecutors. There has been no evidence to support this complaint. Indeed, the same argument could be made against assigned private counsel. After all, it could be argued that the trial judge decides what the assigned attorney is paid, and this makes the assigned attorney too "cooperative" with the court and thus not aggressive enough in promoting his client's interests.[22]

The public defender system is in full and effective force in seven judicial districts. I believe that it should be expanded. Expansion into districts where it would be most cost effective is now being cautiously considered. I agree with the Courts Commission, which in its recommendation to expand the public defender system where it would be cost effective said: "In the final analysis, however, the court system belongs to the public, and it is their best interest that should be served. If that best interest requires a public defender system to provide some of the legal representation for indigents, the preference of the bar and bench must be secondary." •

---

21. *Op. cit. supra* note 4.

---

22. For example, a superior court judge recently complained to an assistant public defender

that it was a waste of state money to have the closing arguments in a jury trial recorded. The court complained that the public defenders regularly moved for recordation whereas the private lawyers did not. A privately assigned lawyer could easily yield to this type of judicial pressure, especially if counsel thought that the judge may make a reduced fee award for not succumbing to the judge's wishes.

Managing Prosecution

(continued from page 4)

duce the data. District attorneys can induce police, for example, to make better arrests by periodically providing information—broken down by department, precinct, and officer—to police supervisors about the outcomes of the arrests brought to prosecution.[20] These reports could include information about the frequencies of each major type of outcome and the reasons for dismissals. Information about outcomes of cases could also be given routinely to victims and witnesses. Police, victims, and witnesses are essential to prosecution; they deserve more systematic feedback than they now receive about how their cases turn out.

Basic management improvements like those described above may soon be standard prosecution practice. Guidelines are gradually gaining acceptability, and more statistical information about prosecution is becoming readily available in many states. Why? One apparent reason is that information-processing technology has advanced so much that it has become irresistible even to those who are ordinarily reluctant to modify the familiar way they do business. This technology in turn produces the data that, when analyzed, often make the need for the guidelines more apparent. A second inducement to reform in prosecution management is pressure—from peers in other jurisdictions, from legislative bodies, from budget officials, from the media, and from political opponents. It is simply no longer respectable for a prosecutor to reject sound principles of management or to resist reasonable attempts to structure the exercise of discretion. •

---

20. Interviews conducted in 1979 with 180 police officers who made arrests in two metropolitan jurisdictions (Manhattan and Washington, D.C.) revealed that none of the officers (nor their immediate supervisors) routinely received information about the court outcomes of their arrests. B. FORST, ET AL., *op. cit. supra* note 6.

North Carolina's Fair Sentencing Act: What Have the Results Been?

Stevens H. Clarke

The Institute of Government recently completed a study that assessed the effects of North Carolina's new determinate sentencing law, the Fair Sentencing Act,[1] by comparing the first year of experience under the new act with experience in previous years. The study was done for the Governor's Crime Commission with a grant from the National Institute of Justice.[2] This article summarizes its results.

Generally speaking, the Fair Sentencing Act (FSA) was intended to reduce unjustified variation in felony sentences and to make sentences more predictable, but not necessarily more severe.[3] Briefly, the FSA:
—Applies only to felonies committed on or after July 1, 1981.

—Leaves former wide ranges in possible prison terms unchanged for most felonies (example: zero to ten years for felonious larceny).
—Sets a presumptive (standard) prison term for each felony (example: three years for felonious larceny).
—Establishes certain criteria (aggravating and mitigating factors) that the judge must consider in deciding whether to impose a nonpresumptive prison term.
—Requires judges either to impose the presumptive prison term or to give reasons in writing for imposing a different term unless the sentence is imposed pursuant to a plea bargain approved by the judge.
—Allows judges to do any of the following without giving written reasons: suspend the prison term with or without probation supervision, impose consecutive prison terms for multiple convictions, and grant CYO (committed youthful offender) status to a felon under 21[4] with eligibility for immediate discretionary parole.

—Provides a right of appellate review of a prison term longer than the presumptive term if the sentence was not imposed pursuant to a plea bargain, and facilitates appellate review by requiring a record of reasons for nonpresumptive prison terms.
—Eliminates discretionary parole except for CYOs.
—Provides for deductions of good time and gain time[5] from the prison sentence at fixed statutory rates, subject to much less discretion by prison officials than former law allowed.

During the study, the Institute interviewed a number of prosecutors, judges, and defense attorneys concerning the FSA and its expected and actual effects. Those interviewed made a variety of assertions about the FSA's effect that were tested as hypotheses in the study. Besides the interviews, four sources of data were used: (1) a sample from twelve representative

---

The author is an Institute faculty member whose field is criminal justice.

1. N.C. GEN. STAT. § 14.1; *id.* §§ 15A-1021. -1340.1 through -1340.7, -1380.1, -1380.2, -1414. -1415, -1442, -1444; *id.* § 148-13.

2. Neither of these agencies is responsible for any statement made in this article.

3. See CLARKE & RUBINSKY, NORTH CAROLINA'S FAIR SENTENCING ACT (2d ed. Institute of Government 1981).

4. After this study was completed, the General Assembly raised the CYO age limit to 25 for misdemeanants and certain felons; N.C. Sess. Laws 1983, Ch. 531.

5. Under the FSA, "good time" is a deduction of one day of the sentence for each day spent in prison without major misconduct, and "gain time" is a deduction at various rates set by statute for work or study assignments. See N.C. GEN. STAT. § 15A-1340.7; *id.* § 148-13.

counties,[6] which provided information on court processing of felony defendants—1,325 before the FSA and 1,193 after the FSA; (2) the Department of Correction (DOC) statewide felony sentence sample,[7] which included 9,752 felons convicted in 1979 and 5,707 convicted in 1981-82 subject to the FSA; (3) the release cohort data—information on time served by felons released from prison (1,634 in 1977-78, 1,569 in 1980, and 2,030 in 1981); and (4) the statewide judgment sample, consisting of information from felony judgments issued under the FSA during August 1981-January 1982 for 1,457 convicted felons.

The study investigated the possible direct effects of the FSA on: sentencing procedures; sentencing practices including suspension (probation), imposition of consecutive prison terms for multiple offenses, and granting of CYO status; the frequency of appeals and post-conviction motions; severity of sentence; and the state prison population. It was possible that the prosecutor and other participants in the processing of felony cases in criminal court could have evaded the policies of the FSA by exercising their discretion to file multiple charges, dismiss and reduce charges, and engage in plea bargaining (including bargaining about the sentence). Consequently, the study also examined multiple charging, dismissal and reduction of charges, and plea bargaining. Court delay was measured to see whether it increased after the FSA. Finally, statistical tests were made to determine whether any changes occurred after the FSA in the effects of certain other factors that had been shown to affect court disposition and sentences before the FSA, such as: the amount of harm caused by the crime; the defendant's prior criminal record; race, age, and sex; how long the defendant spent in pretrial detention (in jail awaiting disposition); the type of attorney he had (privately paid or court-appointed); and whether he pleaded guilty

6. The twelve counties were Mecklenburg, New Hanover, Buncombe, Rockingham, Craven, Harnett, Rutherford, Anson, Cherokee, Granville, Pasquotank, and Yancey.

7. The DOC felony sentence data included defendants convicted of felonies who received either active prison sentences or supervised probation. It did not include those convicted felons who received other sentences such as unsupervised probation, but these were rare (estimated at no more than 10 per cent of the total).

or opted for a jury trial. The results are summarized below.

Multiple charging

In a sense, the FSA provides an incentive (albeit unintentional) to file multiple felony charges against a defendant: no written findings need be made by the judge (nor evidence provided by the prosecutor to support them) to impose consecutive presumptive sentences for each charge, although imposing a longer-than-presumptive sentence for any single charge would require findings and supporting evidence. But the twelve-county sample indicated no increase in the number of felony charges per defendant; in fact, this number declined from 1.90 to 1.56. The use of consecutive sentences grew, but this did not result in longer total sentences after the FSA than before.

Trial court dispositions

Some court officials thought that the FSA, by setting what they considered rather low presumptive prison terms for felonies, would remove some of the incentive to plead guilty because defendants would believe that these presumptive terms would limit what they would receive if they gambled on a trial and were convicted. But this did not occur. The twelve-county data indicated that jury trials dropped from 5.7 per cent of all defendants' dispositions to 3.2 per cent; virtually all the decrease occurred in jury felony convictions (see Table 1). The rate of guilty pleas remained almost constant (59 per cent pre-FSA, 58 per cent post-FSA), but a shift occurred after FSA toward pleading guilty with a formal (recorded) plea bargain (the latter rate increased from 33 per cent to 39 per cent) rather than pleading guilty to the original charge or pleading guilty with an "informal" bargain or understanding. Meanwhile, the rate of dismissal of all charges increased slightly—from 34 to 37 per cent. To the extent that these changes in trials, plea bargains, and dismissals are attributable to changes in the behavior of prosecutors, defense attorneys, and judges,[8] what may

8. The changes in disposition patterns were not necessarily due to any change in the behavior of prosecutors, defense attorneys, and judges caused by the FSA; they could have been due to

have happened (and this is speculative) is that some defendants who formerly would have gone to trial and been convicted of felonies by juries were, after the FSA, pleading guilty pursuant to formal plea bargain. (Another possible explanation—but much less plausible—is that those who would formerly have been convicted of felonies by juries were, after the FSA, having all their charges dismissed.)

Some knowledgeable observers had predicted that sentence bargaining—negotiation of plea bargains in which the prosecutor agrees to make a sentence recommendation desired by the defendant—would increase after the FSA, because imposing the plea-bargained sentence requires no support in written findings. This prediction also did not come true; in fact, sentence bargaining became less frequent after the FSA. Among defendants who pleaded guilty to felonies pursuant to a formal plea bargain, the percentage who obtained a prosecutor's promise of any sort of sentence recommendation decreased from 59 per cent to 45 per cent.

These results suggest—although they do not conclusively prove—that some defendants who would formerly have gone to a jury trial and been convicted of felonies were, after the FSA, pleading guilty pursuant to a formal plea bargain. They also suggest that felony defendants were more willing, after the FSA, to plead guilty to felony charges without the added assurance of a prosecutor's sentence recommendation; this result may have been due to the increased predictability of sentence lengths under the FSA. On the other hand, the decline in felony sentence bargaining may have been part of a growing distaste for the practice that had nothing to do with the FSA.

Examination of disposition patterns among the twelve individual counties indicated that, while the counties retained the individual differences observed before the FSA, they experienced the same overall shifts: jury trials became less frequent with most of the decrease occurring in felony guilty verdicts, written plea bargains increased, other guilty pleas declined, and dismissal rates generally increased somewhat.

mere chance variation, or to small changes with respect to strength of evidence, severity of crimes, and the like in felony cases coming into the court system.

Trial court delay

Concern was expressed before the FSA went into effect that it would increase the time necessary to dispose of felony cases in trial courts, both by making sentencing procedure more complicated and by removing some of the defendant's incentive to plead guilty. In reality, trial court disposition times *decreased* in the twelve counties studied but not necessarily because of the FSA. The median time from arrest to disposition declined from 58 days pre-FSA to 48 days post-FSA, and the 75th percentile decreased from 117 days to 104 days. This speeding up of dispositions seems to result from the reduction in the frequency of jury trials after the FSA plus the slight increase in dismissals. Sentencing procedure ap-

parently did not become much more time-consuming. probably because judicial findings were rarely required to support sentences.

Sentencing procedure

The statewide judgment sample indicated that after the FSA. judges gave written reasons to support the sentences of only 17 per cent of defendants convicted of felonies. Fifty-four per cent of defendants convicted of felonies received presumptive prison terms, and another 22 per cent were sentenced according to a plea bargain; neither of these kinds of sentences requires judges to give reasons. Sentences of another 5 per cent of the felons were unsupported by judicial findings without any explanation stated on the judgment.

When judges did give reasons, aggravating circumstances outweighed mitigating factors somewhat more often than the reverse. Judges, when they did make written findings, tended to cite as reasons for their sentences the defendant's prior convictions (or absence thereof), his voluntary acknowledgment of wrongdoing to a police officer, the fact that he committed the offense for hire or pecuniary gain, a mitigating mental or physical condition, and good character or reputation—all of which were specifically listed in the FSA and could be cited simply by checking appropriate boxes on the judgment form. But in about 20 per cent of the cases in which written findings were made, judges exercised their authority under the FSA to find aggravating or mitigating circumstances not specifically listed in the new legislation.

Judges had been expected to order written presentence reports by probation officers more frequently after the FSA, because of the FSA's emphasis on certain specific aggravating and mitigating circumstances as criteria in sentencing. But the twelve-county data indicated that presentence reports became *less* frequent, dropping from 7 per cent of cases in which defendants were convicted of felonies to only 1 per cent. Court-ordered presentence diagnostic commitments to prison for psychiatric examination also continued to be rare after the FSA. Perhaps judges saw no need for sentencing information other than what the prosecution and defense provided, or perhaps they had little confidence in presentence investigations.

Table 1

Twelve counties: Court Dispositions of Felony Defendants* Before and After Passage of the Fair Sentencing Act

	Before FSA (1970-80)		After FSA (1981-82)	
	Percentage	N	Percentage	N
District Court				
Dismissed, PJC, or deferred prosecution	26.68%	(346)	31.09%	(369)
Voluntary dismissal by prosecutor	19.51	(253)	23.84	(283)
Dismissal with leave by prosecutor	0.93	(12)	.42	(5)
Dismissal by judge	6.17	(80)	4.97	(59)
PJC	0.08	(1)	0.42	(5)
Deferred prosecution	0.00	(0)	1.43	(17)
Pleaded guilty to misdemeanor	21.28	(276)	20.89	(248)
Plea bargain on record	5.63	(73)	7.92	(94)
Other guilty plea	15.65	(203)	12.97	(154)
District-court trial	1.08	(14)	0.76	(9)
Acquittal	0.54	(7)	0.25	(3)
Misdemeanor conviction	0.54	(7)	0.51	(6)
Grand Jury				
"No true bill"	0.62	(8)	0.51	(6)
Went to superior court	50.35	(635)	46.76	(555)
Superior Court				
Dismissed, PJC, or deferred prosecution	7.09	(92)	6.40	(76)
Voluntary dismissal by prosecutor	5.47	(71)	4.97	(59)
Dismissal with leave by prosecutor	0.85	(11)	0.42	(5)
Dismissal by judge	0.62	(8)	0.34	(4)
PJC	0.15	(2)	0.59	(7)
Deferred prosecution	0.00	(0)	0.08	(1)
Pleaded guilty	37.55	(487)	37.15	(441)
Plea bargain on record	26.45	(343)	31.26	(371)
Pleaded guilty to misdemeanor	8.17	(106)	8.26	(98)
Pleaded guilty to felony	18.27	(237)	23.00	(273)
Other guilty plea	11.10	(144)	5.90	(70)
Pleaded guilty to misdemeanor	2.08	(27)	0.93	(11)
Pleaded guilty to felony	9.02	(117)	4.97	(59)
Superior court trial	5.71	(74)	3.20	(38)
Acquittal or mistrial	1.08	(14)	1.01	(12)
Conviction	4.63	(60)	2.19	(26)
Misdemeanor conviction	0.31	(4)	0.34	(4)
Felony conviction	4.32	(56)	1.85	(22)
Total Felony Defendants	100.0%	(1,297)	100.0%	(1,187)

*Includes defendants whose cases began by arrest or summons; excludes those whose cases began by direct indictment or transfer from juvenile court.

Probation, consecutive prison terms, and CYO commitment

Since the FSA does not require written reasons for (a) imposing probation (i.e., suspending a prison sentence), (b) imposing consecutive prison terms for multiple felonies, and (c) committing the offender to prison as a CYO with immediate eligibility for discretionary parole, many might might be exercised more frequently after the FSA as a way to evade its requirements of judicial findings to support nonpresumptive prison terms and its abolition of discretionary parole for non-CYOs. In reality, probation did not increase. Supervised probation with no active time to serve dropped from 45 per cent to 37 per cent of those convicted of felonies, and "special probation" (with a short period of time to serve as a condition of suspending a longer prison term) remained at 4 per cent. (These and other results derived from the DOC statewide sentence sample do not include the felons—estimated at no more than 10 per cent of the total convicted—who received neither active prison sentences nor supervised probation.) CYO commitments also did not increase, still being imposed in 49 per cent of the sentences to prison of felons under 21. Consecutive sentences did increase substantially, according to the 12-county data—from 18 per cent before the FSA among felons who received multiple active sentences to 32 per cent after the FSA. But total sentence lengths generally did not increase after the FSA (in fact, they became shorter), and multivariate analysis of the DOC data indicated that the number of felony convictions for which the person was sentenced influenced his total prison term no more after the FSA than it had before. Consecutive sentencing may have been used to a greater extent after the FSA to circumvent the act's requirement of written findings to support nonpresumptive prison sentences, but it did not generally result in greater severity of sentence.

Severity and variation in sentencing

The twelve-county data indicated that there was no increase after the FSA in the likelihood that defendants *charged with* felonies who were convicted of some charge (half the time a misdemeanor) would receive an active (i.e. unsuspend-ed) prison sentence. But for defendants *convicted of* felonies statewide, the DOC data indicated that the chance of receiving an active prison sentence (rather than supervised probation) increased from 55 per cent in 1979 (pre-FSA) to 63 per cent in 1981-82 (post-FSA). Multiple regression analysis indicated that the post-FSA increase in the probability of receiving an active prison sentence persisted when other variables (such as type of offense and prior convictions) that might have been responsible for the change were controlled for. Whether the increase in active sentencing was attributable to the FSA is open to question, because the FSA left the decision to suspend a prison sentence completely in the judge's discretion. The increase in active sentences may have resulted from a change in judicial attitudes that had nothing to do with the FSA, or it may have been the psychological result of the FSA's presumptive prison terms for felonies, which judges may have regarded as legislative recommendations for *active* prison terms.

With regard to the length of active prison terms imposed for felonies, *sentencing became less severe after the FSA, and it also varied less* (see Figure 1). Before the FSA, total active maximum prison terms had a mean of 121 months and a median of 60 months; after the FSA, total active prison terms had a mean of 82 months and a median of 36 months. The interquartile range[9] dropped from 36-120 months before the FSA to 24-72 months after the FSA, indicating a reduction in variation. Similar reductions in means, medians, and interquartile ranges were found for most of the common specific felonies. *The median sentence length imposed under the FSA was equal to the presumptive prison term in most cases.* The drop in length of active sentence for felonies was confirmed by multiple regression analyses of the DOC data, both when only active sentences were included and when supervised probation sentences were added and treated as having zero length.

Because the law regarding service of prison terms was changed by the FSA—discretionary parole was abolished except for CYOs, and good time and gain time were made statutory—separate analyses were made that compared the time actual-

Figure 1

DOC Statewide Felony Sentence Sample: Distribution of Total Active Maximum Sentence Lengths Before and After FSA—All Felonies

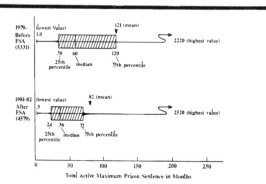

Explanation: Shaded box shows interquartile range (from 25th to 75th percentile); vertical line in shaded box shows median; black triangle shows mean; and horizontal line shows full range.

9. The interquartile range is the range from the 25th percentile to the 75th percentile, sometimes called the "middle 50 per cent" of the range.

ly served by felons released from prison in 1977-78, 1980, and 1981 with estimates[10] of time served on FSA active sentences imposed in 1981-82. Considering the 20 most frequent felonies of conviction, time served in prison will generally decrease and vary less for those sentenced after the FSA than for those sentenced under prior law, although the changes are in most cases not confirmed by statistical significance tests. For two felonies—second-degree murder and armed robbery—time served will apparently increase and vary more after the FSA, but this fact probably results from legislative changes that preceded the FSA rather than from the FSA itself.

Other variables

The study indicated that the defendant's prior convictions and the degree of physical injury and property loss caused by his crime had no more influence on severity of sentence after the FSA than before, despite the fact that the FSA emphasized these variables as aggravating factors. But the effect of other variables did change somewhat after the FSA, according to the regression analysis of the DOC data on felony sentences.

Whether an active sentence was imposed. The chance of receiving active time for violent felonies dropped somewhat (compared with the chance of receiving an active sentence for theft[11] felonies) after the FSA went into effect, although the change was significant only at the .10 level.[12] Some change may have

occurred in the effects of age, sex, and race, but it could not be confirmed by tests of statistical significance. Defendants under 21 and female defendants, who before the FSA were significantly less likely than older defendants and male defendants (respectively) to receive active sentences, were closer to those defendants in the probability that they would receive an active sentence after the FSA; and black defendants, who were significantly more likely than whites to receive active time before the FSA, were not as much more likely than whites to receive active time after the FSA.

Length of active sentence. Drug felony sentences became longer (relative to theft felony sentences) after the FSA. (This change may be due, at least in part, to legislation,[13] effective July 1, 1980, that set very long minimum sentences for the fairly infrequent "trafficking" offenses—those involving large amounts of drugs.) The disadvantage of black defendants apparently nearly disappeared after the FSA. Before the FSA, the felony active sentences of blacks were estimated to be 7.8 months longer than whites' sentences; the difference dropped to nearly nothing after the FSA (this change was significant only at the .10 level). Time spent in pretrial detention, which was positively associated with length of active sentence, showed a slightly decreased effect after the FSA.

"Overall" length of active sentence (including supervised probation sentences as zero). After the FSA, drug felony overall sentences became longer (perhaps partly because of the new "drug trafficking" punishment) and violent felony overall sentences became shorter relative to sentences for theft felonies like breaking and entering and larceny. Thus the FSA overall sentences for the *most severely punished* (violent) felonies tended to *decrease* relative to sentences for theft felonies, and sentences for the *least severely punished* felonies (drug offenses) tended to *increase* relative to sentences for theft felonies. Black defendants' overall sentences became shorter relative to whites' (although this interaction effect was significant only at the .10 level).

Administrative variables. The FSA apparently did not change the in-

fluences on sentencing of how long the defendant spent in pretrial detention and whether he had a court-appointed attorney, but it may have changed the influence on sentencing of a guilty plea. (These administrative variables were tested in multiple regression models using the twelve-county data, which included felony defendants who were convicted of reduced misdemeanor charges as well as those who were convicted of felonies.) That the FSA had little effect on the influence of pretrial detention and type of attorney is not surprising, because the legislation did not attempt to change pretrial release or defense of indigents.

Both before and after the FSA, the longer a defendant spent in pretrial detention, other things being equal, the greater the odds were that he would receive an active prison sentence and the longer his overall active sentence was likely to be. (For example, for defendants convicted of felonies under the FSA who received active prison sentences, the regression model estimated that the length of the active sentence increased by about two months for each additional ten days spent in pretrial detention.) Time in pretrial detention varied a great deal among defendants and apparently had very little to do with the seriousness of their charges, their prior criminal records, and other "risk factors" in their cases—at least insofar as these factors could be measured from available data. One reasonable explanation of the observed correlation between pretrial detention time and severity of sentence is that spending time in detention made defendants less able to help their attorneys prepare arguments for a nonprison sentence, less able to maintain employment and otherwise favorably impress the sentencing judge, and more willing to accept an unfavorable plea bargain offered by the prosecution.[14]

---

10. Time served on sentences imposed under the FSA is much easier to estimate than time served on sentences imposed under former law, because the uncertainty of discretionary parole has been removed and good time and gain time are much more predictable. A good rough estimate of the time actually served on an FSA prison term is 40 per cent of the term. A more precise estimate—the one used in the Institute's study—can be obtained from a formula derived by Kenneth Parker of the DOC's research staff.

11. Theft felonies—used for comparison purposes because they are the most common type of felonies—are here defined to include felonious larceny, breaking or entering of buildings, and receiving and possessing stolen goods.

12. "Significant at the .10 level" means that the observed change had no greater than a 10 per cent chance of being an accidental result of sampling. The significance level normally used in statistical analysis is .05.

---

13. N.C. Gen. Stat. § 90-95(h).

---

14. The study results that show a positive association between pretrial detention time and sentence severity, controlling for other factors, may be explainable in other ways [see Clarke et al., Felony Prosecution and Sentencing in North Carolina 26-28, 38-39 (Institute of Government, University of North Carolina, May 1982)]. Tests were made to determine whether pretrial detention time and severity of sentence were both determined by other variables such as the defendant's dangerousness as perceived by judicial officials—in other words, whether the correlation between pretrial detention and severity of sentence was spurious. The tentative conclusion

Among theft felony defendants who were convicted of some charge, those with court-appointed counsel continued after the FSA to be more likely to receive active sentences and to receive much longer overall sentences than those who paid their attorneys themselves. Pleading guilty rather than going to trial continued to be advantageous for theft felony defendants after the FSA, as it had been before the FSA, in that it was associated with shorter overall active sentences when other relevant factors were controlled for statistically. But for violent felony defendants, the differential in overall length of sentence between those who pleaded guilty and those who went to trial apparently disappeared after the FSA (the change was significant only at the .10 level). This change may have been due to (1) the decline in formal plea bargains concerning the sentence that occurred after the FSA, (2) ceasing the practice of granting more lenient sentences to those who pled guilty, or (3) the reduced proportion of jury trials resulting in felony convictions. These factors could, in turn, have been caused by the FSA, but we cannot be sure.

---

was that the correlation was not spurious—or not entirely spurious—because of these results: (1) Separate regression analyses indicated that very little of the variance in detention time could be explained by the "dangerousness factors" that could be measured from available data, like criminal record and type of charge. In other words, even among defendants who were similarly situated with respect to charge, criminal record, evidence, degree of harm caused to the victim, and other variables that could be measured, there were great differences in pretrial detention time. (2) In any case, the regression analysis that showed the association between detention time and severity of sentence *controlled statistically for* other variables that might have explained this association. The study's finding about detention time can also be interpreted as being attributable to incomplete or inaccurate measurement of "dangerousness" factors that could have explained away the apparent link between detention time and severity of sentence—for example, the information that police, prosecutors, and judges had concerning defendants' criminal histories that did not appear in the local records used for the Institute's study. This interpretation is probably correct to some extent, although the measurements of "dangerousness factors" that were used in the study *did* explain a substantial amount of the variation in severity of sentence, which suggests that they captured at least part of reality. I conclude that some, at least, of the correlation between detention and sentence severity is due to an independent effect of detention on sentencing, as the text of this article explains.

Effect on prison population

In looking for possible effects of the FSA on the state's already rapidly increasing prison population, the study explored this question: Given the number of persons convicted of felonies, how will the FSA affect their contribution to the prison population? Two trends had to be reconciled: (1) The probability of receiving an active prison sentence for a felony *rose* after the FSA (this increase was not a strictly legal effect of the FSA, but it may have resulted from a psychological effect); and (2) the length of active prison sentences and estimated time served in prison generally *decreased*. Times served for several common felonies under pre-FSA law (adjusted for the pre-FSA active sentence rates) were compared with estimated times served under the FSA (adjusted for the higher active sentence rates now generally prevailing). The comparisons indicate that those convicted will contribute less to the prison population under the FSA than they would have contributed if they had been sentenced under former law. A similar analysis was done for all felonies taken together, with the same result.

The DOC has recently completed two forecasts of the prison population.[15] One uses the estimated times served under the FSA, and the other uses the longer times served under previous law. They indicate that by 1986 the prison population will be about 900 inmates less with the FSA in effect than it would have been if previous laws and parole practices had remained in place. These estimates and forecasts indicate that the FSA will probably not increase the felon prison population and may even reduce it somewhat.

O n balance, it is fair to conclude from this study that the FSA accomplished at least some of what it was intended to accomplish, and without creating the problems that critics predicted it would create. Length of active sentences for felonies clearly varied less after the FSA. The fact that the FSA presumptive prison term was generally the median length of active sentence is strong evidence that the reduced variation was

---

15. KENNETH PARKER, PRISON POPULATION PROJECTIONS THROUGH 1986 (North Carolina Department of Correction. Research Bulletin No. 14. Raleigh, N.C.: July 13, 1983.)

due to the FSA. Further evidence of adherence to the FSA's presumptive prison terms is the fact that judges tended to impose these terms even though they were generally well below the pre-FSA median and mean prison terms. Thus, although much variation remained in sentence lengths, the tendency was toward greater consistency.

While judges varied less in the length of active sentence for felonies, according to our statistical analysis they did not become more sensitive to aggravating factors emphasized by the FSA, such as prior convictions, degree of physical injury, and amount of property loss. Perhaps it was unrealistic to expect judges to comply equally with the two somewhat conflicting directives that the FSA gave them. In effect the FSA told judges: (1) adhere to standard sentences and justify nonstandard sentences in writing; but (2) pay more attention to certain specific aggravating and mitigating circumstances. Judges were apparently better able to implement the first directive than the second. The use of presentence investigations, which were expected to increase under the FSA because of the emphasis on aggravating and mitigating factors, in fact declined. (There are no data on whether the prosecution and defense supplied better sentencing information to judges when the FSA went into effect.) In only 17 per cent of the felony sentences did judges actually state in writing aggravating or mitigating circumstances to support the sentence, owing to both the frequent use of presumptives and sentence bargaining. But 17 per cent can also be regarded as better than nothing. Before the FSA, judges were never required to support their sentences with reasons—and in fact did so at their peril, since recorded reasons invited appellate review and reversal.

The study results with regard to race were encouraging: there were indications that the disadvantages of black defendants in sentencing declined or disappeared after the FSA. Perhaps these disadvantages had less influence on severity of sentence simply because sentences varied less.

The FSA still leaves some large loopholes in the exercise of prosecutorial and judicial discretion, which provided much opportunity to evade the policies of the legislation. But by and large, little evasion seems to have taken place through these loopholes. For example, multiple

(continued on page 40)

The Judicial Standards Commission—
Assuring the Competence and Integrity of North Carolina Judges

Gerald Arnold

T he conduct of public officials has received a great deal of publicity in recent years, and judges no less than others have been in the public eye. Although most judges are honest, competent, and diligent, the few exceptions make the headlines.

North Carolinians should be aware that the General Statutes and the Code of Judicial Conduct drawn up by the State Supreme Court require judges to maintain certain standards of conduct. Public confidence in the judiciary is an indispensable ingredient of the rule of law. Before people can have that confidence, they must know that when judicial misconduct or disability does occur, there is an independent, impartial body to recommend that the errant judge be disciplined or the disabled judge removed. That is the job of the North Carolina Judicial Standards Commission.

History of the Commission

The Commission came into existence in January 1973, after the voters approved an amendment to the State Con-

stitution two months earlier. That amendment, along with legislation to implement it, had been proposed by the North Carolina Courts Commission.[1] It was designed to provide a new method of removing or censuring judges. Before the amendment was adopted, North Carolina had only two methods for removing judges: (1) address—that is, removal for "mental or physical incapacity by joint resolution of two-thirds of all the members of each house of the General Assembly,"[2] and (2) impeachment—that is, removal through accusation by the House of Representatives and trial by the Senate.[3] There was no way at all to discipline a judge short of removing him. Both systems had proved ineffective—no judge had been removed by impeachment since 1868, and address had apparently never been used.[4]

The amendment (N.C. Const. art. IV, § 17 sec. 2) and implementing legislation (G.S. Ch. 7A, Art. 30) provide that on the Judicial Standards Commission's recom-

The author is a judge of the North Carolina Court of Appeals and Chairman of the Judicial Standards Commission.

1. NORTH CAROLINA COURTS COMMISSION, REPORT TO THE NORTH CAROLINA GENERAL ASSEMBLY 19 (1971).
2. N.C. CONST. art. IV. § 17 (1).
3. Id.
4. Op. cit. supra note 1.

mendation to the State Supreme Court, a judge may be censured or removed on any of the following grounds:[5]

(1) Willful misconduct in office;
(2) Willful and persistent failure to perform his duties;
(3) Habitual intemperance;
(4) Conviction of a crime involving moral turpitude;
(5) Conduct prejudicial to the administration of justice that brings the judicial office into disrepute;
(6) Mental or physical incapacity interfering with the performance of the judge's duties and is, or is likely to become, permanent.

To provide judges with notice of what conduct is expected of them, the State Supreme Court[6] adopted the North Carolina Code of Judicial Conduct.[7]

Most cases that have reached the Supreme Court involved the first and fifth items on the above list. An example of willful misconduct in office would be taking money to dispose of a case in a certain manner. That act would also be conduct prejudicial to the administration of justice. Embezzlement is an example of a crime involving moral turpitude.

The Judicial Standards Commission has the heavy responsibility of carrying out these constitutional and statutory provisions. It has seven members[8]—three judges, two lawyers, and two laymen—who serve six-year overlapping terms without pay except for expenses. They may not serve more than one term. The judges—all appointed by the Chief Justice of the Supreme Court—include a Court of Appeals judge, who serves as Commission Chairman, a superior court judge, and a district court judge. The lawyers, who must have practiced for at least ten years, are appointed by the State Bar Council. The citizen members, who must be laymen, are appointed by the Governor.

The Commission also has a three-member permanent staff—an executive secretary (who is a lawyer), an investigator, and a secretary.

The Commission at work

Most complaints that reach the Commission allege errors in judges' decisions, evidentiary rulings, and judgments[9] but do not allege misconduct. For example, a disappointed litigant in a domestic case may claim that the judge would not let his witness testify. Such alleged errors may be corrected on appeal, and the Commission has no jurisdiction to consider them. The Commission is exclusively concerned with the six grounds for removal or censure listed above, and it follows the Code of Judicial Conduct as a guide in applying the statutory provisions for disciplining judges.[10]

In regard to these six bases for discipline, the Commission may institute an investigation upon a written complaint by a citizen or on its own motion.[11] If preliminary investigation shows that further proceedings are warranted, it files a formal complaint and a hearing is held, after which the Commission may recommend disciplinary action to the Supreme Court. If the Commission decides not to file a formal complaint, it may still issue a private reprimand to the respondent judge.[12]

A Commission proceeding is not a trial that results in a sentence. Supreme Court Justice James Exum described the nature of a Commission inquiry in a 1975 case:

> This proceeding is neither criminal nor civil in nature: It is an inquiry into the conduct of a judicial officer, the purpose of which is not primarily to punish any individual but to maintain due and proper administration of justice in our State's courts, public confidence in its judicial system, and the honor and integrity of its judges.[13]

The proceedings before the Commission and the papers filed with it are confidential, unless the judge being scrutinized requests otherwise. But the Commission's recommendation to the Supreme Court and the record sup-

---

5. N.C. Gen. Stat. § 7A-376.

6. As authorized by N.C. Gen. Stat. § 7A-10.1.

7. Id. Vol. 4A. Appendix VII-A. The Code contains seven canons and specific rules under each one. The canons are broad principles. For example, Canon 2 states: "A judge Should Avoid Impropriety and the Appearance of Impropriety in All His Activities." Regulation B under Canon 2 says. "A judge should not allow his family, social, or other relationships to influence his judicial conduct or judgment."

8. The current members include the author, Judges Douglas Albright and L. T. Hammond, Jr., E. K. Powe. Jerome Clark. Susan Whittington. and Veatrice Davis.

---

9. See Figure 1 for statistics through the end of 1982. Less than 2 per cent of the complaints filed with the Commission have resulted in a recommendation to the Supreme Court. Over 560 complaints had been filed through March 1983: of these. only nine resulted in a Commission recommendation to the Supreme Court. See TENTH ANNUAL REPORT OF THE NORTH CAROLINA JUDICIAL STANDARDS COMMISSION (1982) for the latest published statistics.

10. The Commission is also guided by the Supreme Court's past action on its recommendations. though since 1973 only nine opinions have been published on these matters. In re Crutchfield. 289 N.C. 597, 223 S.E.2d 822 (1975); In re Edens, 290 N.C. 299, 226 S.E.2d 5 (1976); In re Stuhl. 292 N.C. 379, 233 S.E.2d 562 (1977); In re Nowell. 293 N.C. 235, 237 S.E.2d 246 (1977); In re Hardy, 294 N.C. 90, 240 S.E.2d 367 (1978); In re Martin. 295 N.C. 291, 245 S.E.2d 766 (1978); In re Peoples. 296 N.C. 109, 250 S.E.2d 890 (1978); In re Martin. 302 N.C. 299, 275 S.E.2d 412 (1982); In re Hunt. _____ N.C. _____. 302 S.E.2d 235 (1983).

11. The Commission's procedures prescribed by statute appear in N.C. Gen. Stat. Ch. 7A. Art. 30. The Commission's own more detailed procedures are published in 17 N.C. App. (appendix), 1972-73. with amendments in Volumes 27 and 34.

12. A censure is a public reprimand issued by the Supreme Court. The Commission may issue a private reprimand on its own authority. A private reprimand goes to the respondent judge to inform him of the Commission's view of such conduct and the consequences that may follow any repetition.

13. In re Crutchfield. 289 N.C. 597, 602, 223 S.E.2d 822, 825 (1975).

porting it are not confidential. They are filed with the Supreme Court Clerk and are open for public inspection.

At least five members of the Commission must concur in any recommendation to the Court. When the Commission recommends that a judge be disciplined, the respondent is entitled to petition the Supreme Court for a hearing on the recommendation, to present a brief, and to argue his case before the Court. If the judge does not petition for a hearing, the Court considers and acts on the Commission's recommendation on the record: failure to petition waives the right to file a brief and to be heard on oral argument.[14]

The Court may approve the Commission's recommendation, send it back for further proceedings, or reject it. A majority of the Court's members who vote must concur in any censure or removal. Of the Commission's nine recommendations for censure or removal through June 1983, the Court has approved eight.[15]

The method of disciplining Supreme Court justices is similar to the one used for disciplining other judges, except that the Commission's recommendation goes to the Court of Appeals. The seven senior judges on the Court of Appeals, excluding the judge who is the Commission chairman, decide on any action to be taken.

Table 1 shows the Commission's procedure. Of 551 complaints filed from 1973 to 1982, the Commission found that it had no jurisdiction in 374 (68 per cent), usually because the alleged misconduct was actually an alleged legal error that should be corrected by appellate review. Twenty-four (4 per cent) of the complaints are still pending, and 70 (13 per cent) were not investigated because they clearly were frivolous or otherwise lacked merit. Eighty-three complaints (15 per cent of the original 551) proceeded to preliminary investigation by the Commission; 68 separate investigations were conducted, some of which involved more than one complaint. Thirty-four (50 per cent) of the 68 investigations led to no further action, and two are still pending; six (9 per cent) resulted in the respondent's leaving office; four (6 per cent) were disposed of by private reprimand; and 22 (32 per cent of the investigations) resulted in the Commission's issuing a formal complaint. Of these 22 cases, seven resulted in private reprimand, one is still pending, and 14 went on to hearings. Eight of the 14 hearings resulted in recommendations of disciplinary action to the Supreme Court; three led to no further action; one resulted in private reprimand; one led to vacation of office; and one is still pending. Of the eight cases recommended for action by the Supreme

Table 1

Summary of Commission Activities: 1973-82

(551 complaints)
Written Complaint by Citizen or Commission
No Jurisdiction (374)
Pending (24)
No Investigation (70)

(83 complaints investigated = 68 separate investigations)[1]
Preliminary Investigation by Commission
No Further Action (34)
Private Reprimand (4)
Pending (2)
Office Vacated (6)

Formal Complaint Filed by the Judicial Standards Commission (22)[2]
No Further Action (6)
Private Reprimand (7)
Office Vacated (0)
Pending (1)

Hearing by Commission (14)
No Further Action (3)
Private Reprimand (1)
Office Vacated (1)
Pending (1)

Recommendation (8)
Supreme Court
No Action (0)
Public Censure (6)
Removal (2)

Source: Tenth Annual Report of the Judicial Standards Commission of North Carolina (1982). Contains statistics through December 31, 1982.
1. Some investigations involved more than one complaint.
2. Preliminary investigations are covered by these formal proceedings.

Court, two resulted in removal from office, and six resulted in public censure without removal. Of the 68 cases investigated in that nine-year period, two (3 per cent) resulted in removal from office, seven (10 per cent) resulted in the respondent's leaving office, and 12 (18 per cent) resulted in private censure.[16]

Suggestions for improvement

Although the Commission has always worked effectively, opening its formal hearings might improve its operation still further. At present the hearing is open only if the respondent judge requests it.[17]

14. Appendix V-A to Volume 4A of the General Statutes: Rule 2(c) of Rules for Supreme Court Review of Recommendations of the Judicial Standards commission.

15. The Court merely censured the respondent in *In re* Martin, 295 N.C. 291, 245 S.E.2d 766 (1978), a case in which the Commission recommended removal. The judge was later removed but for different conduct from that involved in the 1978 case. *See In re* Martin, 302 N.C. 299, S.E.2d 412 (1981).

16. Since this article was written, the Commission has recommended that a superior court judge be removed, and the Supreme Court is now reviewing that recommendation.

17. *See* N.C. GEN. STAT. § 7A-377(a).

A former member of the Court of Appeals and former chairman of the Commission, Edward B. Clark, recently pointed out how the confidentiality requirement works:

> [E]xperience has revealed that when the formal complaint has been filed and subpoenas issued, the nature of the charges and the Commission hearing become known to the public and the news media. Confidentiality beyond the point when the formal complaint is filed results in reduced public confidence and deprives judges of the accurate information as to the proper limits of judicial discretion.[18]

Still, some phases of the proceedings clearly must be confidential. The overwhelming majority of complaints against judges are frivolous and unfounded, and a judge's reputation should not be damaged by publicizing such charges.

At present, nothing becomes public until the Commission files its recommendation with the Supreme Court. In my opinion, it would be better to allow the inquiry to be made public when the formal complaint that sets the stage for the formal hearing is filed. Since the Commission screens unfounded complaints before it decides whether to file a formal complaint,[19] the likelihood of damage to the reputation of a judge who did no wrong is small—a baseless claim would not reach the public hearing stage.

Before the Commission or any other public institution can be legitimated, it must be seen. Benjamin Disraeli once commented, "Without publicity there can be no public support, and without public support every nation must decay." By holding hearings in public, the Commission makes its presence known, and it avoids any possible accusation that it conducts Star Chamber proceedings. It is fair to say that justice is the public's business and that respect for the process could be improved by public hearings.

Conclusion

Although few North Carolina judges will ever be the subject of a formal misconduct complaint by the Judicial Standards Commission, it is critically important that the few misconduct complaints that are issued be dealt with in a manner publicly perceived as fair and just. Public understanding of the Commission and its role in overseeing the conduct of our state's judges is important to the effective operation of the Commission and to the judicial system as a whole. As Chief Justice Charles Evans Hughes once stated, "[N]o man is as essential to his country's well-being as is the unstained dignity of the courts." •

18. Clark. *The Discipline and Removal of Judges in North Carolina*. 4 CAMPBELL L. REV. 1, 20 (1981).

19. See Figure 1. The Commission has filed a formal complaint in only 4 per cent of the initial complaints. Thus only 4 per cent of Commission hearings would have been open if this suggested improvement had been in

effect. As noted in footnote 9, *supra*, only 2 per cent of the initial complaints received have resulted in a recommendation to the Supreme Court.

The Solar Transition in North Carolina

Richard D. Ducker

A recent technological and economic trend that has gone largely unnoticed has been the increased use of solar energy in North Carolina. Today over 3,000 passive solar homes, 2,000 domestic solar water-heating systems, and 300 active solar space-heating systems are being used in this state. Solar power is providing industrial process heat at several industrial sites (for example, the Cone Mills' Cliffside textile plant), and local governments are also using solar energy systems. The new Mount Airy Public Library incorporates a passive solar design that has dramatically reduced the lighting, heating, and cooling costs generally associated with buildings of that size and type. Wilson now uses a "solar still" for treating sludge in its wastewater treatment facility, and Chapel Hill's new public safety building has both passive heating and cooling features and a solar water-heating system.

In addition, some North Carolina communities have used federal funds to retrofit low- and moderate-income housing and other private buildings for solar applications. Shelby, Jacksonville, High Point, and Fuquay-Varina have incorporated solar water-heating systems or simple solar space-heating units (window boxes) into their Community Development Block Grant rehabilitation projects.

The state's largest sponsor of office-building construction, state government itself, is not now legally required to evaluate the feasibility of incorporating passive solar design in new buildings, but the Office of State Construction has developed a series of passive solar designs for certain proposed state buildings on an experimental basis.

Several state buildings already use solar energy, including a highway patrol office and a driver's license center in Anson County, a highway welcome center in Surry County, and additions to buildings on the North Carolina State and North Carolina Central University campuses.

Several state programs that encourage the use of solar energy merit special attention. Funded under the Federal Energy Extension Service, the North Carolina "Solar Spec" Program was organized by the North Carolina Division of Energy (in the Department of Commerce) to encourage builders and developers to incorporate passive solar heating and cooling designs into their house plans for use in the residential speculative market. The program provided free technical assistance, including the services of a qualified architect. In 1980 and 1981 the Solar Spec program directly assisted 10-15 per cent of the state's speculative builders, and passive solar design features were incorporated into more than 200 individual house plans. It is estimated that as a result of this program, over 1,400 homes with solar features will be built. The Energy Division has also offered design, marketing, and financing workshops for lenders, realtors, developers, and appraisers to acquaint them better with solar development. This winter the Division will offer builders and the public a set of 12 passive solar house plans specifically designed for North Carolina.

One very successful promotion was the Governor's Showcase of Solar Homes during 1981-82. Sponsored jointly by the Energy Division and the Alternative Energy Corporation (about this organization, more in a moment), this program attracted over 23,000 North Carolinians to visit 109 solar homes located in 81 counties. Fifty-three of these homes were valued in the $30,000-$50,000 range, and 46 at between $50,000 and $80,000.

The author is an Institute faculty member whose fields include planning and land use.

One problem for the solar industry is that too few qualified laborers and craftsmen are familiar with solar design, materials, and construction. Recent experience suggests that problems with solar systems come more often from poor installation than from the equipment itself. In an effort to provide skilled workmen, the North Carolina State Department of Public Instruction has begun pilot programs in at least nine high schools to teach installation, servicing, and maintenance of solar systems. In addition, several state universities and a number of community colleges now offer more advanced courses in solar technology.

North Carolina has also benefited from the Solar Home Program of the Farmers' Home Administration (FmHA), an agency of the U.S. Department of Agriculture. (See the article on FmHA by John Vogt in the Summer 1981 issue of *Popular Government*.) Because of this state's rural nature, FmHA has been an important source of mortgage loan money and loan guarantees in North Carolina. In the past several years it has encouraged the use of solar energy. To date FmHA has financed over 1,000 solar homes and 10 passive solar apartment complexes in over 90 North Carolina counties.

Perhaps the state's most unusual institutional advocate of solar in North Carolina is the Alternative Energy Corporation. It was established in 1980 pursuant to an order of the State Public Utilities Commission after a series of public hearings indicated a need for a statewide program to encourage more widespread use of alternative energy management technologies. The Commission proposed that all of the state's suppliers and distributors of electrical power form a nonprofit corporation for this purpose. Duke Power, Carolina Power and Light, Virginia Electric and Power, ElectriCities of North Carolina, Nantahala Power and Light, and the North Carolina Electric Membership Corporation all joined. Seven members of the Corporation's board of governors are appointed by the Governor to represent the public interest; the other six are named by the contributing organizations.

The Alternative Energy Corporation (AEC) is supported by members' contributions, which are proportionate to the amount of electricity used by the respective contributors' ratepayers. Recently, annual contributions have been pegged at 45 cents per ratepayer, so that the organization has an annual budget of about $2.2 million.

The AEC's mission is to reduce peak demand for electricity and moderate the growth in demand for electrical power by encouraging use of cost-effective renewable energy systems, load management systems, and conservation. Much of the AEC's research is directed toward evaluating the performance and cost of renewables and toward marketing and financing them. Its charter calls for the AEC to expire on December 31, 1985.

Cost comparisons

How competitive are solar energy systems in cost? The economics of installing a solar system is likely to be a substantial factor in any consumer's decision to "go solar." But for the consumer, comparing solar costs with the costs of alternate sources is often difficult. According to the Alternative Energy Corporation, "Until the means for making such comparisons are readily available and widely accepted many people will continue to choose familiar conventional technologies—even when an alternative system is the better choice." For this reason utility companies may have little incentive to facilitate such comparisons. Any comparison must contend with a multitude of economic variables: the present and future prices of competing fuels and sources of power, the reliability and efficiency of the primary systems (and any backup systems), their maintenance costs, the peculiarities of the building or lot, the means available for financing, the differences and peculiarities among solar products of the same type, and availability of tax incentives.

Still, a few general conclusions about costs seem warranted, and they suggest that one should conserve energy first and then consider alternative energy sources. The most cost-effective steps that most property owners can take are to insulate hotwater heaters, caulk doors and windows, put up storm windows, lower thermostats, install fans, and use the scores of procedures available to reduce energy consumption. Passive solar design is often the best next step. One major study indicates that passive solar designs compare more favorably in cost with electric-resistance, natural gas, and fuel oil systems than would comparable designs that rely on active solar space heating.[1] It also suggests

---

SOLAR TERMINOLOGY

Solar energy: energy transmitted from the sun in the form of electromagnetic radiation

Active solar systems: systems that incorporate mechanical means or moving parts such as motors, valves, or pumps to operate (e.g., most solar water-heating systems)

Passive solar systems: systems that incorporate structural design features rather than mechanical devices to collect, transfer, and store solar energy

Solar collectors: plates or other materials that capture and accumulate solar radiation for subsequent transfer to other parts of the system

Photovoltaics: the process for converting solar radiation directly into electricity.

---

1. Fred Roach, Scott Noll, and Shaul Ben-David, "The Comparative Economics of Selected Passive Solar Designs in Residential Space Heating Applications," abstracted from *Prospects for Solar Energy: The Impact of the National Energy Plan* (Los Alamos, N.M.: Los Alamos Scientific Laboratory, December 1977).

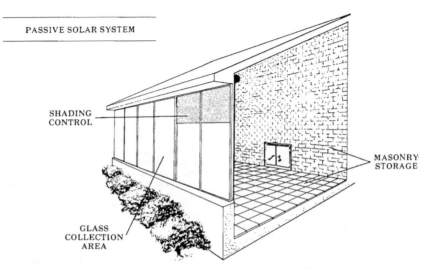

PASSIVE SOLAR SYSTEM

SHADING
CONTROL

MASONRY
STORAGE

GLASS
COLLECTION
AREA

Source for illustrations: John Manual. *Sunbook: A Guide to Solar Energy In North Carolina* (Raleigh. N.C.: North Carolina Department of Commerce, undated).

that North Carolina may be one of the few states in the country where, by 1985-90, a house designed for passive solar energy may be a better energy value than a gas-heated house.

A study conducted in 1979 for the public staff of the State Utilities Commission concluded that even under the set of forecasting assumptions most unfavorable to solar, solar water-heating systems were more economical than electric-resistance water-heating systems.[2] But at present active solar water- and space-heating systems are not competitive with heating systems based on either electric heat pumps or natural gas.

The factor that makes solar energy systems increasingly competitive is tax credits, which are available from both the federal government and the State of North Carolina for the installation of solar equipment. The current federal credit allows a taxpayer who installs solar equipment in either his current or new home a credit equal to 40 per cent of his installation expenses up to $4,000. Virtually all components of an active system qualify. However, eligibility requirements for elements of a passive solar system are strict. The elements may not serve a "dual purpose" (serve a structural as well as solar function for the building). Federal tax law also allows a business a 15 per

cent tax credit for installation of active (not passive) solar equipment in addition to the regular 10 per cent business investment tax credit that was already available.

North Carolina provides personal and corporate income tax credits of up to 25 per cent of eligible expenditures for active solar systems that qualify under federal law and for certain passive systems to a maximum of $1,000 per system on any one building. The state also offers a

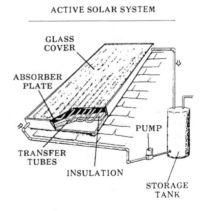

ACTIVE SOLAR SYSTEM

GLASS
COVER

ABSORBER
PLATE

PUMP

TRANSFER
TUBES

INSULATION

STORAGE
TANK

2. *Impacts of Load Control. Solar Heating, Industrial Cogeneration. Conservation. and Time-of-Day Rates on Utility Loads and Generating Requirements in North Carolina*, report prepared by ICF. Inc. for the North Carolina Utilities Commission Public Staff. Raleigh, May 1979.

20 per cent credit ($8,000 maximum) for installation of solar equipment used in producing heat for manufacturing processes. Finally, it offers the "solar property tax exemption" that prohibits the appraisal of a solar system for ad valorem tax purposes at a value greater than the value of a conventional heating or cooling system, even though it may have cost more.

Without tax credits, a property owner's rate of return on a solar investment would not make solar energy appear very attractive. Such an investment for a typical home or business is likely to require a considerable outlay of money. For example, a new active solar hot-water system for a single-family house may cost from $3,000 to $4,000, and combination active space- and water-heating systems generally cost from $5,000 to $13,000. Passive solar design features may cost from several hundred dollars to thousands. Nevertheless, most consumers seem to expect that they will recover their investment relatively quickly. In a study made by the Harvard Business School, 80 per cent of the respondents suggested that they would not think seriously about buying an active solar heating system if it did not return their investment within two years—which most solar systems will not do. However, when the discounted cash flows that result over the entire life of a solar system are calculated, the system will generally compare favorably in cost with other energy sources.

Another crucial factor in comparing energy systems is how a solar investment is financed. Unless some sort of subsidized loan program is available to the property owner, the interest rate and term of a loan secured by a first mortgage on a new building will generally be more attractive than any financing arrangement that the owner of existing property may be able to secure. For this reason, it is less costly to incorporate either a passive design or an active system into a new building than to retrofit the same system into an existing building. For existing buildings, home improvement loans made by local financial institutions or second mortgages may be the only financing available.

The cost effectiveness of solar systems is often compared with that of conventional electric-resistance systems. This comparison is complicated by the fact that most solar systems require a backup source of power or fuel for periods without sustained sunshine because their storage capacities are limited. That backup system is often electrically powered; therefore the electric rates that apply when it is used are important. The proponents of both solar energy and conventional electric power claim that inequities in the pricing of backup electric power distort proper comparisons between the two systems.

Some solar advocates claim that "all-electric" rates discriminate unjustly against solar energy. These promotional rates are offered to residential consumers who rely almost exclusively on electric power. When "all-electric" rates are used, the electric rates charged to owners of solar systems when they use their backup systems may exceed the rates charged "all-electric" customers for the same

period of use. Those who favor solar suggest that if promotional rates are used at all, they should favor backup service for solar systems since the use of alternative energy sources will decrease the overall demand for electric power. "All-electric" rates still apply to many utility customers in North Carolina; but the Utilities Commission is now phasing them out, and the utilities under its jurisdiction may no longer offer them to new customers.

Others claim that owners of solar systems do not pay their share of the costs that electric utilities incur in providing the backup service. Energy conservation advocates have generally called for utilities to offer "peak hour" or "time-of-use" pricing. Such pricing systems require customers who use electricity during periods of heaviest demand to bear the costs of providing the additional plant and equipment necessary to generate and distribute power during these periods. They do, however, offer kilowatt-hour charges lower than regular rates during hours of lesser demand. Duke Power, Virginia Electric Power, and Carolina Power and Light all offer "time-of-use" pricing on a voluntary basis to some or all of their customers. Few owners of electric solar backup systems are likely to choose this option. Electric solar backup systems are often used during periods of peak electric demand—for example, on cold winter mornings. Since "time-of-use" pricing is not mandatory and special "demand charges" (designed to recover the fixed costs of providing plant and equipment to service peak loads) are not imposed on residential customers, critics claim that users of electric backup systems may not bear an appropriate share of the cost of serving them. However, as the storage and holding capacities of solar systems are increased so that backup systems are used less frequently or are used only during off-peak hours, any possible pricing inequity that exists is likely to become less significant.

The Task Force on Solar Law

The North Carolina Energy Policy Act of 1975 created the Energy Policy Council to advise the Governor and the General Assembly on matters of energy policy. In 1981 the Council recommended to the Governor that he name a Task Force on Solar Law to determine the nature of the legal and institutional barriers to the full development of solar energy in North Carolina. It specified that the task force be made up of people with a wide range of expertise in solar design and building, finance and taxation, utility and land-use law, and government. In April 1982 the Governor appointed a task force of twelve regular members and nine advisory members selected from agencies and institutions of state government.

This fall the Task Force is expected to complete its work and present recommendations in a report to the Governor that will also include a package of legislative proposals. Its major recommendations and proposals are summarized below.

Task force recommendations on utilities. One dilemma of public policy affecting solar energy is what role electric utility companies should play in solar development. To provide electricity, utilities typically rely on a system that is based on a monopoly market, substantial investment in plant and equipment, and centralized decision-making. Utilities have heretofore been seen as the sole producers and converters of energy, and some of them are likely to perceive solar and other alternative systems of energy as a threat. Nonetheless, their cooperation, support, and increased direct involvement is probably essential to solar development. Utilities can play an important role in marketing solar and other alternative technologies, perhaps even in installing and maintaining equipment. On the other hand, the entry of utilities into these solar markets may threaten independent solar suppliers and installers.

Recognizing these problems, the Task Force determined that North Carolina's utilities should be encouraged to invest in alternative energy systems in a manner consistent with free-market competition and principles of fair trade. Legislation proposed by the Task Force directs the North Carolina Public Utilities Commission to promote energy conservation and "all feasible uses of alternative energy supply sources." More important, those proposals direct the Commission to encourage the public utilities to supply and install residential alternative energy and conservation devices (defined broadly to include virtually all solar systems) to the "fullest extent allowed . . . by Federal law." The proposals also place limits on the activities of public utilities. A utility is not allowed to engage in unfair methods of competition or to provide any supplier or contractor with an "unreasonably large share" of contracts to supply or install solar and related energy conservation equipment. Similarly, whatever financing the utility makes available for systems installed by approved contractors must also be available to consumers who install their own system.

Under the proposed legislation, the Utilities Commission is directed to study the potential impact of electric rates on the backup service (typically electric) that is generally necessary for solar and other alternative energy systems. It is also to study thermal storage devices (generally a part of any solar system) that can reduce the peak loads of public utilities. A vital feature of the legislation requires the Commission to establish rates to encourage residential use of energy conservation measures (including solar systems).

To encourage public utilities to invest in "centralized" alternative energy facilities (including those that rely on solar, biomass, wind, and geothermal technologies), the Commission would be authorized to grant a higher rate of return on such an investment than would otherwise be permitted. According to the Task Force, the measure recognizes the additional public benefits of alternative energy facilities, their typically benign environmental impact, their reliance on resources indigenous to the state, and their favorable impact on utility loads.

The Task Force also wished to make it possible for solar facilities and projects to be financed with industrial revenue bonds issued by local governments. Since the North Carolina Constitution prohibits the use of these bonds for "public utilities," the proposed legislation also contains technical amendments to the effect that small

Mount Airy
Public Library

(courtesy of J. N. Pease Associates)

power producers and other small alternative energy facilities (including solar) are not to be treated as "public utilities." Other provisions specifically provide that counties may issue revenue bonds for industrial and agricultural facilities that incorporate solar energy systems.

Task Force recommendations on financing. The Task Force found that one significant barrier to increased use of solar energy was poor financing arrangements for the installation of solar systems. Low-interest, long-term financing arrangements that correspond to the life-cycle benefits of such systems are often not available in North Carolina for those who wish to install residential systems, particularly for buildings that require retrofiting. The Task Force found that many lenders, appraisers, and realtors are unfamiliar with solar systems and that traditional lending practices are typically not applied when loans are made for solar systems. Further, the interest rate and terms of loans that ordinarily apply to home improvements are not attractive enough to encourage solar investment.

To solve these financing problems, the Task Force recommended that the North Carolina State Housing Finance Agency and the various utilities be authorized to assume new roles in solar financing. Legislation proposed by the Task Force would authorize the Housing Finance Agency to make mortgage or energy-conservation loans to primary lenders from funds generated by the sale of tax-exempt energy revenue bonds. It would also be authorized to purchase pre-approved mortgage or energy conservation loans made by lenders to sponsors of residential housing or made directly to owners of low- and moderate-income housing. Under the proposed legislation, a third function of the Agency would be to purchase residential mortgage loans that it has not approved in advance on condition that the lender use the proceeds of the sale to make loans to benefit low- and moderate-income persons. In any case, however, the proceeds from the Agency's direct loans or loan purchases could be used for energy-related loans only if the Agency determined that the energy-related loans would not otherwise be available from private lenders on "reasonably equivalent terms and conditions." That restriction is designed to ensure that the Agency's revenue bonds qualify for tax-exempt status and the proceeds from Agency loans and purchases are spent for a public purpose, as the State Constitution requires. The Task Force anticipates that the Agency will set an income ceiling for recipients of loans derived from the sale of tax-free bonds.

The Task Force recommends that state utilities assume a complementary role in providing low-interest loans for solar installations. Costs of such loans could be reduced and the credibility of solar investment enhanced if utilities originated and administered solar loans, established standards for solar installers and solar equipment, and used present information-disseminating, billing, and servicing procedures for this purpose. Furthermore, the Task Force

recommends that the utilities provide insurance as additional security for the loans, perhaps through bad-debt reserves. They could thus distribute the risks and costs of such insurance by treating it as an expense in the rate formula.

Task Force recommendations on solar access. One major risk associated with installing equipment is loss of access to the sun. The sun's rays strike the earth (and solar collectors) at angles. As a result, most sunlight must ordinarily pass through neighboring airspace before it can be collected. No consumer should consider a solar system without some assurance that the necessary sunlight will not be obstructed. Of course, many North Carolina solar buildings are located on lots large enough and on terrain flat or barren enough so that neighbors' trees and buildings will not block needed sunlight. In many urban areas, however, the feasibility of solar systems in certain locations is substantially limited by problems of solar access.

The Task Force's recommended legislation is designed to offer private property owners and units of government several legal tools for dealing with such problems. One legislative proposal recognizes "solar energy easements" as interests in real property and establishes basic criteria and guidelines for creating them. The Task Force anticipates that such easements, so defined, will become the primary method for establishing a "solar right" through privately negotiated agreements. But not all private restrictions on land use are favorable to solar energy. The legislation recommended by the Task Force provides that restrictive covenants and similar provisions in deeds and land sales contracts that effectively prohibit a reasonably sited and designed solar energy system from being installed are void because they are contrary to public policy.

The solar access proposals also authorize cities and counties to use their present land-use regulatory tools (particularly subdivision and zoning regulations) to protect solar access and encourage energy conservation measures in new development. Under this proposal, local governments would have explicit authority to regulate the height and location of trees as well as buildings in order to protect solar access. Another controversial recommendation would empower local governments to require land subdividers to establish solar access easements for those subdivision lots for which a solar system is feasible. Finally, the Task Force recommends giving municipalities and the State Division of Highways the power to trim trees and to regulate the selection and location of trees within street and highway rights-of-way in order to protect solar access.

It is too soon to evaluate the reaction of the General Assembly and the general public to these Task Force recommendations. Few of the ideas suggested have been subject to substantial public debate, and many North Carolinians are unaware of the potential that solar and other alternative energy systems offer right now. Thus the primary purpose of disseminating the Task Force's report will be educational. The adoption of the Task Force recommendations could substantially hasten the development of solar energy in North Carolina and amount to fuller recognition of the role that the state and local governments can play in energy matters. In any case, these recommendations should lay the groundwork for the development of public policies to guide a solar transition that is already well under way in this state. •

Bibliography

Annual Report 1981-82. Research Triangle Park, N.C.: North Carolina Alternative Energy Corporation, November 1982.

Ball, David. "Return on Investment for Residential Solar Water Heating." Southern Solar Energy Center, Atlanta, January, 1981.

Daly, Les. "A Latter-day Icarus Tries to Build his Solar Dream House," *Smithsonian* 12, no. 6, (September 1981), 131-38.

Deudney, Daniel, and Christopher Flavin. *Renewable Energy: The Power to Chose.* Worldwatch Institute Book Series. New York: W. W. Norton and Co., 1983.

"Impacts of Load Control, Solar Heating, Industrial Cogeneration, Conservation and Time-of-Day Rates on Utility Loads and Generating Requirements in North Carolina," Report prepared by ICF, Inc., for the North Carolina Utilities Commission Public Staff, Raleigh, N.C.: May 1979.

Gimlin, Hoyt, ed. *Energy Issues: New Directions and Goals* (Editorial Research Reports). Washington, D.C.: Congressional Quarterly, Inc., 1982. Chapter 4, "Solar Energy's Uneasy Transition."

Gumz, Gary. *The North Carolina Renewable Energy Directory.* Raleigh, N.C.: North Carolina Coalition for Renewable Energy Resources. Spring 1982.

Manuel, John. *Governor's Showcase of Solar Homes: Final Report,* Raleigh, N.C.: North Carolina Department of Commerce, Energy Division. 1983.

Manuel, John. *Sunbook: A Guide to Solar Energy in North Carolina.* Raleigh, N.C.: North Carolina Department of Commerce, Energy Division, undated.

1980-81 Energy Report. Raleigh: North Carolina Energy Policy Council, September 1982.

North Carolina Energy Institute. *1981 Annual Report.* Raleigh, N.C.: 1982.

Parker, Jon. *The North Carolina Book of Renewable Energy Projects.* Durham: North Carolina Coalition for Renewable Energy Resources and North Carolina Land Trustees of America, Fall 1982.

Roach, Fred, Scott Noll, and Shaul Ben-David. "The Comparative Economics of Selected Passive Solar Designs in Residential Space Heating Applications." abstracted from *Prospects for Solar Energy: The Impact of the National Energy Plan.* Los Alamos, N.M.: Los Alamos Scientific Laboratory, December 1977.

Rodberg, Leonard, and Meg Schacter. *State Conservation and Solar Energy Tax Programs: Incentives or Windfalls?* Studies in Renewable Resource Policy. Washington, D.C.: Council of State Planning Agencies, 1980.

The Solar Lobby and the Center for Renewable Resources. *The Solar Agenda: Progress and Prospects.* Washington, D.C.: May 1982.

The Smart Home. Raleigh, N.C.: Astron Technologies, undated.

Stoubaugh, Robert, and Daniel Yergin, eds. *Energy Future: Report of the Energy Project at the Harvard Business School.* 3d edition. New York: Ballentine Books, 1983. Chapter 7, "Solar America."

Controlling Hazardous Wastes: What Are the Options?

Alvis Turner

What makes a waste hazardous? How much hazardous waste is generated, and where does it go? How can hazardous wastes be dealt with, and specifically what can North Carolina do to manage and control them? This article explores these questions.

1980 was a legislative landmark in hazardous waste management.[1] In that year the U.S. Environmental Protection Agency (EPA) published[2] the Hazardous Waste and Consolidated Permit Regulations under the Resource Conservation and Recovery Act[3] and Congress passed the Comprehensive Environmental Response, Compensation and Liability Act[4]—better known as Superfund. Congress had enacted the Resource Con-

servation and Recovery Act (RCRA) in 1976. The regulations that were part of that law (Subtitle C) did not completely address the hazardous waste problem, since they primarily concern permits for and proper management of present and future hazardous waste disposal sites. Superfund was intended to deal with the many substantiated and potential hazards posed by thousands of abandoned and uncontrolled sites across the nation that have resulted from the casual disposal of hazardous wastes decades ago.

What is a hazardous waste?

One principal reason for EPA's delay in promulgating hazardous waste regulations after RCRA was passed was the need to establish specific criteria or measurable characteristics that could be used to identify a waste as hazardous. Such a definition is crucial to an effective hazardous waste management effort. The 1980 regulations define as hazardous any waste that has one or more of the following characteristics:

Corrosive—highly acidic or highly alkaline;
Ignitable—potentially a fire hazard;

The author is a member of the Environmental Science and Engineering faculty in the School of Public Health at the University of North Carolina at Chapel Hill.

1. In a 1980 survey across the nation, the Environmental Protection Agency documented 350 uncontrolled hazardous waste sites that could present substantial threats to the public. More than 15,000 of these uncontrolled sites are now listed in EPA's *Emergency Response and Information System*, published by the Congressional Office of Technology Assessment (Washington, 1983).
2. U.S. Environmental Protection Agency, Hazardous Waste and Consolidated Permit Regulations. 40 CFR Part 260, *Federal Register*, May 19, 1980. *Ibid. Hazardous Waste Generation and Commercial Hazardous Waste Management Capacity: An Assessment*. Office of Solid Waste. Publication no. 894 (December 1980).
3. P.L. 94-580.
4. P.L. 96-510.

Reactive—capable of exploding or releasing toxic gases; and

Toxic—capable of producing acute or chronic effects harmful to man or the environment.

The regulations also include standardized tests that can be used to determine whether a substance exhibits any of these characteristics.

Some wastes that have relatively low hazard levels and are usually produced in high volume are specifically exempted from regulation as hazardous. These include fly ash, mining wastes, domestic sewage discharged into publicly owned treatment works, waste burned as fuel, and hospital wastes. EPA is now considering the need to regulate infectious wastes from medical care facilities.

How much waste? And where does it go?

One major function of any management process is to gather and organize information that is both accurate and sufficient to permit problems and goals to be defined. EPA's hazardous waste regulations addressed this function by requiring that all *large* hazardous waste generators—those that produce more than 1,000 kilograms per month—submit an annual report to EPA or the state (in this article, a "generator" is an industry that generates hazardous wastes); the first designated reporting period was calendar year 1981. This requirement has been changed, and reporting will now be required of only a statistical sample of large generators. But many states have passed more stringent regulations that still require annual reporting by all large generators. The data generated by these annual reports are essential for an effective and sound state management system. In my opinion, North Carolina should also seriously consider requiring a modified and concise annual report from all of the state's *small* generators of hazardous waste.

The following data were collected in the state's annual survey of hazardous wastes for 1981.[5] In that year approximately 394 million pounds (178,685 metric tons) of regulated hazardous waste were generated in North Carolina, and another 3.3 million pounds (1,497 metric tons) were brought into the state. Since reporting was not required of small generators (those that produce less than 1,000 kilograms per month), perhaps 20 million more pounds were generated but not reported.[6] If North Carolina's experience is like the nation's, the reported hazardous wastes accounted for approximately 10 to 15 per

cent of all industrial waste generated in the state in 1981.[7]

Nationwide, 70 to 80 per cent of all hazardous waste is managed on the sites where it is generated.[8] In 1981, 65 per cent of all such waste generated in North Carolina was managed on the generator's site and approximately 20 per cent was shipped elsewhere. The remainder—15 per cent, or 60 million pounds—was stored, treated, or disposed of off-site but within the state. Only 7 per cent of the regulated hazardous waste was placed in landfills.[9]

Management and control

No single technique or method now available or expected in the near future will provide for the safe management of all hazardous waste. This waste may be in the form of solids, liquids, gases, or complex mixtures of a number of phases. In 1980[10] EPA estimated that chemical hazardous wastes are 39 per cent solids, 33 per cent sludges, 15 per cent chemical solutions, 7 per cent solvents, and 6 per cent oils. A variety of methods and options will be necessary to manage these wastes in an environmentally sound manner (see Figure 1).

Land disposal. On a volume basis, most hazardous waste (as much as 80 per cent, according to early EPA data) is disposed of on land—deep-well injection, lagoons, and landfills. In Texas, 95 per cent of hazardous wastes are disposed of in this way.[11] Disposal on land costs less than other disposal options. A recent assessment in California[12] concluded that it would cost approximately $50 million per year to recycle, treat, and destroy all of California's high-priority wastes, including pesticide wastes, polychlorinated biphenyls (PCBs), cyanide wastes, toxic metal wastes, halogenated organics, and nonhalogenated volatile organics—an increase of about $33 million over the current annual cost in California of land disposal. These estimates include care and monitoring of landfills for 30 years after closure, as required by RCRA. But they do not include the cost of clean-up or compensation for damage to human health and the environment if the system should fail after 30 years; nor do they include the cost of the permanent loss of a natural resource like groundwater.

Landfills and underground injection wells are containment technologies aimed at perpetual storage. They are

---

5. Solid and Hazardous Waste Management Branch, Division of Health Services, North Carolina Department of Human Resources, *North Carolina 1981 Annual Report of Hazardous Waste* (Raleigh, N.C., 1982).

6. Office of Technology Assessment, Congress of the United States, *Technologies and Management Strategies for Hazardous Waste Control* (Washington, March 1983) (henceforth OTA, *Technologies and Management Strategies*).

7. T. H. Maugh, "Burial Is the Last Resort for Hazardous Wastes," *Science* 204 (1979), 819.

8. OTA, *Technologies and Management Strategies*.

9. Tracor Jitco, *An Analysis of North Carolina's Industrial Waste*, (Rockville, Md.: Tracor, Inc., February 17, 1983).

10. *Federal Register*, May 19, 1980.

11. OTA, *Technologies and Management Strategies*.

12. Governor's Office of Appropriate Technology, *Alternatives to the Land Disposal of Hazardous Waste: An Assessment for California* (Sacramento, 1981).

Figure 1

Hazardous Waste Management

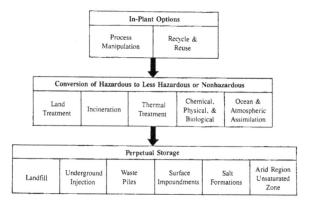

Source: National Research Council Committee on Disposal of Hazardous Industrial Wastes, *Management of Hazardous Industrial Wastes: Research and Development Needs* (Washington, D.C.: National Academy Press, 1983).

intended to inhibit release of hazardous components into the environment, but some releases seem inevitable eventually. The National Research Council Committee on Disposal of Hazardous Industrial Wastes[13] recently said that the 30-year time span established by RCRA as a period of concern for hazardous waste in landfills and perpetual storage options was unrealistic—*500* years is more like it.

If RCRA care and monitoring requirements for land disposal of stable and persistent hazardous wastes were increased from 30 years to even 100 years, the economic incentives associated with land disposal would disappear. But even if the costs of landfilling hazardous wastes doubled or tripled, some form of perpetual storage—either above or below the earth's surface—will probably still be required for certain limited categories of hazardous materials like:

—Low-level radioactive wastes, which must be stored until they decay to natural background levels;

—Ash residues from hazardous waste incinerators, which must be stored to isolate concentrated heavy metals (like cadmium) from the environment;

—Nondegradable and nonleachable solid materials (isolate substances like plastics, which are difficult and expensive to treat or incinerate);

—Spill and clean-up debris (low-toxicity, high-volume, primarily inert materials).

Above-ground storage of hazardous wastes is not a realistic option. Retrieving and detoxifying these wastes at some future date is an alchemist's dream. Storage, either above or below ground, is likely to lead to attempts at perpetual containment, which merely postpones the problem and the costs of safe disposal for future generations. A sound state policy would prohibit the containment of persistent, mobile, and highly toxic waste.

Treatment. For wastes characterized as hazardous because of their reactivity, corrosiveness, and ignitability, well-established chemical and physical treatments are available. Such wastes can be chemically neutralized, incinerated, or oxidized. The major disincentive to these treatment technologies is economic. The costs of (1) constructing and operating facilities for these processes, (2) segregating some wastes at the point of production to insure effective and safe treatment later, and (3) disposing of some residuals can be substantial. However, it is wiser to absorb these near-term costs than to transfer the costs to the future (when they will have become much greater) and to risk the unacceptable health and environmental effects associated with land disposal of these hazardous materials.

Such wastes are most often treated physically or chemically, but highly toxic wastes can also be treated biologically. An important issue in managing toxic con-

13. National Research Council Committee on Disposal of Hazardous Industrial Wastes. *Management of Hazardous Wastes: Research and Development Needs* (Washington. D.C.: National Academy Press, 1983).

stituents (which may be organic, inorganic, or metallic) is to describe the nature and impact of potential releases—whatever the chosen treatment technology may be. Incineration may destroy 99.99 per cent of a constituent, but the total amount of the constituent released and its toxic effects still must be considered. For example, even with a destruction efficiency of 99.99 per cent, the incineration of 100,000 pounds of a toxic waste could release 10 pounds of the material into the atmosphere, which would be totally unacceptable for substances like PCBs. The destruction or detoxification efficiency of biological treatment is usually much less than 99.99 per cent. This fact reinforces the point, which cannot be made too strongly, that while treatment is the preferred alternative to land disposal of toxic wastes, direct control and monitoring of the industrial processes that generate wastes will be essential to prevent environmental discharges that may present unacceptable levels of risk for human health. Preventing generation of hazardous wastes is more effective than attempting to dispose of the wastes.

EPA regulations do not prohibit the land disposal of corrosive, reactive, and ignitable wastes if steps are taken at the landfill to prevent reaction or ignition, and they do not permit regulatory agencies to ban chemicals from disposal sites on toxicological grounds. In order to discourage land disposal, individual states will have to promulgate their own regulations. States that do so should also provide technical and siting assistance and tax incentives to the private sector to encourage the construction of treatment facilities comprehensive enough to manage these wastes adequately. Siting of hazardous waste facilities is a major problem everywhere. The public generally views risks associated with *any* nearby facility as unacceptable—or uncertain, at best. Since these uncertainties make private-sector commitments of capital difficult to obtain, state and local government assistance will be crucial for establishing adequate treatment facilities close to generators

so as to minimize transportation costs. Smaller generators of hazardous waste in particular will need these off-site treatment facilities, since the smaller the quantity of waste handled, the greater the per-unit treatment costs. Discouraging or prohibiting the land disposal of hazardous wastes without adequate treatment facilities can only promote unsafe (and perhaps illegal) management practices and limit industrial growth.

Reduction of wastes. Several technological approaches can be used to reduce the amount of wastes that require treatment or disposal.[14] These include:
—Separating wastes. Keeping wastes in concentrated, isolated forms rather than producing large-volume indiscriminate mixtures;
—Modifying the process. Making the process more efficient in order to produce fewer residuals (this approach will vary with individual plants and processes);
—Substituting end products. Substituting a different product or improving product performance when a process produces a high volume of hazardous waste (for example, changing from water to solvent dyeing of carpets in the textile industry reduces the amount of wastes, costs, and energy);
—Recycling. Recovering and reusing residuals, either by the generator or by another industry.

While the effort to reduce the generation of hazardous wastes has not had broad success in industry, several companies—most notably the 3M Corporation in the United States—have demonstrated the practical application of the strategies used to effect reduction.[15] Whether

14. OTA, *Technologies and Management Strategies.*
15. L. W. Lehr, "Preventing Pollution Pays Better Than Controlling It," *Financier* 5, no. 12 (December 1981).

A toxic-waste dump
in North Carolina

these approaches will become widespread will depend on the cost of instituting them and the amount of savings that result from having a smaller volume of waste to dispose of. An industry will adopt these initiatives if the cost of reducing generation is less than the cost of treating or disposing of the wastes that would have been produced.

North Carolina could provide an incentive for reducing the generation of waste by increasing the costs of treatment and land disposal. It could do this by requiring comprehensive, stringent monitoring at all hazardous waste management facilities, requiring retrofiting of existing treatment lagoons and landfills, and increasing the requirements for care and monitoring after closure beyond the present 30 years. The state might also apply strict liability (so that anyone who sued would not have to prove negligence on the operator's part in order to collect compensation) to all transporters of hazardous wastes and to all treatment, storage, and disposal facilities. This action would effectively increase the costs of conducting hazardous waste management activities by increasing the cost of liability insurance. It would both encourage reduction of generation and ensure that the cost of transporting, treating, storing, and disposing reflects the true social costs of these activities. But it might also discourage the establishment of adequate transportation and hazardous waste management facilities within the state.

North Carolina already provides some financial support to the Piedmont Waste Exchange (PWE), which operates under the auspices of the Urban Institute at the University of North Carolina at Charlotte. Even though information clearinghouses like PWE have not yet greatly affected the recycling of hazardous wastes, they offer a promising alternative—recycling—to treatment and disposal of these wastes. The state should increase its support to PWE in order to insure that this technique for reducing the amounts of waste to be disposed of will continue.

N orth Carolina is committed to reduction of hazardous waste generation as the best available option for managing these wastes. This policy is clearly stated in the Waste Management Act of 1981:[16] "[The Governor's Waste Management] Board shall periodically . . . make recommendations to the Governor, cognizant State agencies, and the General Assembly on ways to improve waste management; reduce the amount of waste generated; maximize resource recovery, reuse, and conservation; and minimize the amount of hazardous and low-level radioactive waste which must be disposed of."[17] (For hazardous waste legislation enacted in 1983, see the box on the next page.)

Reducing the amounts generated is a fundamental way to reduce threats to public health and the environment from hazardous wastes. But despite reduction efforts, a certain volume of these wastes will inevitably be produced. Once generated, they can be either treated to reduce their level of hazard or disposed of through secure containment on land. Still, land disposal should be reserved exclusively for those wastes or residuals that cannot be economically recycled or cannot be further treated. The ultimate goal should be to reduce land disposal to the smallest possible volume—and to only those wastes that can be stored for hundreds of years without endangering man's health or environment.

North Carolina should consider the following additional strategies for effectively regulating and managing hazardous waste generated in this state.

EPA no longer requires annual reporting even by all large hazardous waste generators, but the state should require annual reports by all generators, both large and small (for small hazardous waste generators, a simplified reporting form could be used). Little information is available on the estimated 336 or more small generators in the state.[18] Sufficient and accurate information is essential for a sound management system.

Protection of groundwater should be a major priority. The state should regularly inspect and require monitoring of groundwater at all existing and new pits, ponds, and lagoons used for industrial waste treatment, storage, or disposal. Many chemicals can be very persistent in groundwater aquifers, and once groundwater is contaminated, corrective action may not be technically or economically feasible.

Adequate physical, chemical, and biological treatment facilities for hazardous wastes should be built within the state. Such construction would aid the state's policy of limiting or excluding land disposal of hazardous wastes. The private sector will need strong technical and siting support from the state and local governments as it seeks alternatives to land disposal of these wastes.

The state's present tax incentives for reducing the volume of hazardous wastes produced should be enhanced by increasing the cost of treatment and disposal through more stringent monitoring requirements and imposing a standard of strict liability and by providing technical assistance to small hazardous waste generators.

The State Department of Human Resources should intensify its efforts in locating, classifying, and cleaning up abandoned and closed hazardous waste sites. County and local governments should actively participate and assist in this task.

16. N.C. GEN. STAT. §§ 130-166.16 et seq.; id. §§ 143B-216.10 et seq.
17. Id. § 143B-216.13(2).

18. G. Dunn, "Should Strict Liability Be Imposed for Injuries Caused by Hazardous Waste?" Revised draft presented to the Governor's Waste Management Board. Solid and Hazardous Waste Management Branch (Raleigh. N.C.. October 22. 1982).

North Carolina Hazardous Waste Legislation 1983

The 1983 General Assembly considered a number of important bills dealing with hazardous wastes, passing some and becoming stalled on others. The legislature made North Carolina a party state (Ch. 714—S 196) in the Southeast Interstate Low-Level Radioactive Waste Management Act (the other states that are eligible for membership in the compact are Alabama, Florida, Georgia, Mississippi, South Carolina, Tennessee, and Virginia). As a member of this interstate compact, North Carolina may continue to use the facility in Barnwell, South Carolina, for disposing of low-level radioactive waste (generally, radioactive waste generated by medical facilities and some of the waste generated by nuclear power plants) until 1993. By that date, the compact must have established one or more other disposal sites in the compact states for use by the member states.

Several new restrictions were placed on the operation of hazardous waste landfills. No hazardous waste landfill or PCB landfill may be placed within 25 miles of any other hazardous waste or PCB landfill (Ch. 605—H 79). Also, hazardous waste and PCB landfills are to be detoxified as soon as the appropriate technology becomes economically available (Ch. 605—H 79). The operator of a hazardous waste landfill must maintain adequate insurance on the facility, as determined by the Governor's Waste Management Board, and must make monthly reports to the Waste Management Board and to the board of commissioners of the county where the facility is located concerning the kinds and amounts of wastes in the landfill (Ch. 546—H 554). The bottom of a hazardous waste landfill must be at least ten feet above the seasonal highwater table—and higher when necessary to protect the public health and the environment (Ch. 564—H 554).

The Legislative Research Commission was authorized to study setting up a program to identify and label toxic substances used in the workplace (Ch. 905—H 1339), and a special Hazardous Waste Study Commission was created to study "alternatives to landfilling hazardous wastes including prevention, reduction, treatment, incineration and recycling." The special commission may report to the 1984 session and must report to the 1985 General Assembly.

Some bills that were not enacted would have imposed strict liability for damage that results from hazardous wastes (H 738), required hazardous waste landfills to be operated only in conjunction with other treatment and management facilities (H 9910), studied the placement of hazardous waste landfills (S 689), and established a clean-up program for abandoned hazardous-substance disposal sites (H 1383). But these bills all passed the house in which they were introduced and therefore may be considered at the 1984 session.

The General Assembly's major effort to limit the types and character of wastes placed in landfills and to impose more stringent requirements on landfill construction than the federal regulations was H 559. The impetus for the bill came from a widely held belief that the EPA requirements regarding the substances that may be placed in landfills and construction of the landfills are not sufficiently stringent and detailed to protect the public health. The difficulty is that G.S. 130-166.21D(b) generally prohibits North Carolina from adopting any stricter or more comprehensive rules regarding hazardous wastes than the federal rules. H 559 addressed these issues and passed both the House and Senate in different versions. A conference committee could not resolve the differences between the two versions before adjournment, but the bill may be considered at the 1984 session. The failure of H 559 to pass leaves North Carolina governed by the current EPA regulations adopted pursuant to the Resource Conservation and Recovery Act. Those regulations do not require clay or other substantial liners in landfills. They also do not require other (non-landfill) treatment possibilities to be exhausted so that landfilling of hazardous substances is used only as a last resort. —**William A. Campbell**

The state should consider expanding the responsibilities of the Governor's Waste Management Board (which are now confined to hazardous and low-level radioactive wastes) to include management of all toxic substances, because the production, use, and disposal of chemical substances are interrelated operations in industrial and agricultural economies. Expanding the oversight and policy functions of the Waste Management Board to include all hazardous substances would be cost effective and would provide an integrated approach to the management of toxic substances.

Hazardous wastes, improperly managed, significantly threaten man's health and his environment. While the rate at which these wastes are generated may decline, the total volume produced will surely increase over the next decade. North Carolina should expand its strategies and options for dealing with these wastes now and in the future.

The Law and Religion in the Public Schools: A Guide for the Perplexed

Benjamin B. Sendor

F ew questions strike the public's emotional chords with the strength of religious activities in the public schools. When this issue arises, school officials find themselves working in an unwelcome spotlight, trying to satisfy two sometimes conflicting masters—public sentiment and legal duty. The intensity and difficulty of resolving controversies over religion in the public schools suggest that a comprehensive guided tour of this question's legal status would be timely.

Let us begin with the source of law governing the relation between government and religion, the First Amendment: "Congress shall make no law respecting an establishment of religion, or prohibiting the free exercise thereof . . . ."

The First Amendment contains two distinct provisions about the relation between government and religion: the free exercise clause and the establishment clause. The Fourteenth Amendment extends these limits on governmental power to state and local governments (including

school districts).[1] The free exercise clause forbids the government from prohibiting the free exercise of religion. Its goal is to keep religious beliefs and practices voluntary, free from government coercion.[2] The establishment clause forbids the federal government from making laws "respecting an establishment of religion." It not only prohibits a government from establishing an official public church but also reaches more broadly to prohibit governmental aid or support of religion, with the aim of separating church and state.[3]

As the Supreme Court has explained, the establishment clause sets forth these principles to shape the relation between government and religion:

Government in our democracy, state and national, must be neutral in matters of religious theory, doctrine, and practice. It may not be hostile to any religion or to the advocacy of no-religion; and it may not aid, foster, or promote one religion or religious theory against another or even against the militant opposite. The First Amendment mandates governmental neutrality between religion and religion, and between religion and nonreligion.[4]

To foster this goal of separation, the Supreme Court has developed a three-part test to determine whether public school policies and activities comply with the establishment clause:

(1) Does the government policy or activity reflect a clearly secular purpose?
(2) Does the activity, as its primary effect, neither advance nor inhibit religion?
(3) Does the activity avoid excessive government entanglement with religion?[5]

A school policy or activity must pass all three parts of the test to survive a challenge under the establishment clause.

The author is a new member of the Institute of Government faculty whose fields include school law. This article is adapted from one that appeared in the July 1983 issue of the *School Law Bulletin*, published by the Institute of Government.

1. School Dist. of Abington Township v. Schempp, 374 U.S. 203, 215-16 (1963); Cantwell v. Connecticut, 310 U.S. 296, 303 (1940). ("The fundamental concept of liberties embodied in [the Fourteenth] Amendment embraces the liberties guaranteed by the First Amendment. The First Amendment declares that Congress shall make no law respecting an establishment of religion or prohibiting the free exercise thereof. The Fourteenth Amendment has rendered the legislatures of the states as incompetent as Congress to enact such laws.")

2. 374 U.S. at 222-23.
3. Schempp, 374 U.S. 203.

4. Epperson v. Arkansas, 393 U.S. 97, 103-4 (1968).
5. Lemon v. Kurtzman, 403 U.S. 602, 612-13 (1971).

The test guides courts in their review, under the establishment clause, of religious activities in public school. It will serve as an analytic compass in this tour of the constitutionality of common religious activities in public school.

The constitutional debate about religion in the public schools historically has focused on the establishment clause rather than on the free exercise clause. This focus stems from the fact that by design most public school religious activities are voluntary for students in order to avoid claims under the free exercise clause that such activities coerce students into abandoning their own beliefs and practices. But the fact that participation in a class and their parents were to approve *dent* is irrelevant to the establishment clause, which is aimed at what the *government*, acting in the form of the *school administration*, does. Even if all students in a class and their parents were to approve of and willingly engage in a religious activity in school, the activity still might run afoul of the establishment clause as improper government support of religion. As the Supreme Court repeatedly has observed, the optional nature of an activity might save a devotional practice from the Scylla of the free exercise clause, but it will not rescue the practice from the Charybdis of the establishment clause.[6]

School prayer

Question: Is audible prayer or Bible reading by or for students constitutional when required or authorized by teachers or school administrators during the school day on school grounds?

Answer: No.

Discussion: The U.S. Supreme Court decisively grappled with the constitutionality of officially sanctioned, audible prayer in public school classrooms in 1962 in *Engel v. Vitale*[7] and again the following year in *School District of Abington Township v. Schempp.*[8] In *Engel* the Court struck down as a violation of the establishment clause the New York public schools' daily classroom recitation of a nondenominational prayer composed by the state government. The law that provided for the devotional permitted students to be ex-

cused from prayer upon parental request. In *Schempp* the Court held unconstitutional, under the establishment clause, a Pennsylvania statute requiring that at least ten Bible verses be read aloud to students without comment at the start of each school day and also a Baltimore policy requiring the recitation of either the Lord's Prayer or a chapter of the Bible without comment at the start of the school day. In both cases the Court found that the laws, policies, and practices at issue failed the first two parts of the three-part test: they had religious purposes, and they advanced the religious beliefs contained in the Bible and in the challenged prayers.

In both cases the Court rejected the assertion that the excusal provisions saved the prayers and the Bible readings. As discussed above, the Court explained that while an effective excusal policy might prevent a religious practice from violating the free exercise clause, it would not save the activity from being a violation of the establishment clause.

Since the *Engel* and *Schempp* decisions, courts across the nation have reviewed statutes and policies that provide for school prayer, only with greater voluntariness than the policies rejected in those cases. For example, in *Kent v. Commissioner of Education,*[9] the Supreme Judicial Court of Massachusetts reviewed a statute requiring teachers to announce at the beginning of each school day a period of prayer to be led by a student volunteer; the law contained an excusal policy. In *Karen B. v. Treen,*[10] the United States Court of Appeals for the Fifth Circuit faced a Louisiana statute authorizing local school boards to permit school officials to allow each classroom teacher to ask at the start of the school day whether any student wished to offer a prayer. If no student volunteered, the statute permitted the teacher to do so. It too had an excusal provision. In *Collins v. Chandler Unified School District,*[11] the United States Court of Appeals for the Ninth Circuit reviewed a policy in an Arizona high school that permitted student council officers to conduct student assemblies in the auditorium during the school day and to begin the assemblies with a prayer. School officials coordinated class schedules to accom-

modate the assemblies. Attendance at the assemblies was optional; students who did not attend were assigned to study hall.

In all three of these cases, the courts declared the challenged practices unconstitutional under the establishment clause, finding that the activities failed all parts of the three-pronged test. They also rejected the argument that the optional nature of the practices should save them from being constitutional violations. Heeding the Supreme Court's lesson in *Engel* and *Schempp*, the courts explained that the voluntary nature of a religious practice does not shield the activity from the establishment clause.

One final point, often lost in the heated debate over school prayer: courts have not banished prayer from the schools, as some critics have charged. They have forbidden only officially sanctioned or sponsored prayer. The establishment clause does not prohibit a student from praying silently or audibly on his own free time during the school day (such as during lunch or recess), provided that his prayer is totally voluntary and unofficial and he does not interfere with other students, teachers, or official school activities. A student on his own time during the school day has as much right to pray privately as he has to ponder a coming test or last night's baseball scores.

Moment of silence

Question: Is an officially sanctioned moment of silence at the start of the school day constitutional?

Answer: There is no clear answer at this time to that question, although most courts that have addressed the issue have struck down moment-of-silence policies.

Discussion: In his concurring opinion in *Schempp*, Justice Brennan suggested that while officially sanctioned audible prayer in public school is unconstitutional under the establishment clause, an officially sanctioned moment of silence might pass muster. He commented that a quiet moment at the beginning of the day might usefully serve to "still the tumult of the playground and start a day of study."[12]

Since Justice Brennan's observations, judicial opinion has been split concerning the constitutionality of official moments of silence in school. In *Gaines*

6. Schempp. 374 U.S. at 220-23; Engel v. Vitale. 370 U.S. 421, 429-30 (1962).

7. Engel. 370 U.S. 421.

8. Schempp. 374 U.S. 203.

9. _____ Mass._____. 402 N.E.2d 1340 (1980).

10. 653 F.2d 897 (5th Cir. 1981).

11. 644 F.2d 759 (9th Cir.). *cert. denied*. 454 U.S. 863 (1981).

12. 374 U.S. at 281 (Brennan, J., concurring).

v. Anderson,[13] a federal district court upheld a Massachusetts statute and a related school board resolution requiring teachers to enforce a period of silence to last not more than one minute at the start of the day "for meditation or prayer." The court analyzed the rule under the first two prongs of the three-part establishment clause test. First, it examined the legislative history of the statute and concluded that the law had a neutral, secular purpose of promoting a reflective atmosphere for study, self-discipline, and respect for authority. The court explained that meditation is not necessarily religious; it encompasses serious reflection about either religious or secular topics. It further noted that the statute's reference to prayer was not constitutionally fatal because it was used in the disjunctive, giving students a choice between meditation and prayer. It then ruled that the enforcement of the statute, accomplished without suggestions from teachers about the appropriate use of the period of silence, neither advanced nor inhibited religion as its primary effect.

In contrast, courts in three recent cases struck down moment-of-silence statutes. In *Jaffree v. Wallace*[14] the Eleventh Circuit invalidated a statute authorizing teachers to begin the first class of the day with a minute of silence "for meditation or voluntary prayer . . . ." The court focused on the intent of the law, finding that the legislative history and the use of the word "prayer" indicated that the law was passed for the religious purpose of returning prayer to the schools.

In *Duffy v. Las Cruces Public Schools*[15] a federal district court held unconstitutional a New Mexico statute that authorized school boards to permit a moment of silence at the start of each day "for contemplation, meditation, or prayer. . ." As in *Jaffree,* the court ruled that the legislative history and the use of the word "prayer" indicated that the law was enacted to bring prayer back to the public schools. The court found that the statute would promote prayer as its primary effect because the public—particularly impressionable children—would perceive the period of silence as a devotional exercise. Finally, the court decided that the statute

would unduly entangle the government in religion through teacher enforcement of the law and political discord in local school districts over the purpose and implementation of the statute.

In *Beck v. McElrath*[16] a federal district court struck down a statute nearly identical to the one challenged in *Gaines* that required teachers to maintain a period of silence not to exceed a minute at the beginning of the day "for meditation or prayer or personal beliefs . . . ." The court ruled that the statute scored failing grades on all parts of the three-part test. First, it examined the statute's legislative history and concluded that it was enacted to inject prayer into the public schools through the constitutional back door under the guise of meditation after the Supreme Court had closed the front door in *Engel* and *Schempp.* Second, it determined that the statute's reference to prayer, together with the absence of guidelines for neutral implementation of the statute by teachers, made it likely that the law's primary effect would be to encourage students to engage in a religious exercise, thereby advancing religion. Third, the court ruled that both the freedom given teachers to interpret the statute and the use of public money to promote a religious exercise (the moment of silence) called for excessive government entanglement with religion.

The judicial conflict over period-of-silence policies leaves few clear guidelines for school officials. At a minimum, the review of the legislative history of the statutes challenged in *Gaines, Jaffree, Duffy,* and *Beck* indicates that courts are likely to declare unconstitutional periods of silence that are intended by either legislatures or school boards as thinly veiled prayer. For example, in *Opinions of the Justices to the House of Representatives,*[17] the Supreme Judicial Court of Massachusetts held that a proposed bill to require teachers to conduct a period of prayer or meditation to be offered by a student volunteer would be unconstitutional. The court distinguished the bill from the statute upheld in *Gaines,* since it would permit a student to lead a class in audible prayer. Courts also are likely to strike down periods of silence implemented by teachers as religious exercises. For example, if a teacher in Massachusetts were to

instruct students, "Be quiet for a minute to pray," even the *Gaines* court probably would declare that teacher's direction unconstitutional. It remains unclear, however, whether a moment of silence instituted solely for secular purposes and enforced by teachers without suggesting that students use the time to pray would be constitutional under the establishment clause.

Student prayer clubs

Question: Is it constitutional for a public school to permit students to form extracurricular clubs to hold group prayer sessions during the school day either before or after class or in free periods?

Answer: Probably not.

Discussion: The constitutionality of student prayer clubs has been a thorny issue for courts and school officials in recent years. Thwarted by court decisions barring officially sanctioned prayer during class time, some students have sought permission to form extracurricular clubs to hold group prayer meetings. Before the Supreme Court's 1981 decision in *Widmar v. Vincent,*[18] a court in *Reed v. Van Hoven*[19] upheld a school policy to permit voluntary student prayer meetings for a few minutes before classes began, as long as the sessions were not held in homerooms and the teachers had no role in selecting the prayers. The court reasoned that such voluntary gatherings, separate from official school activities and from teachers' control over the content, were a lawful accommodation of government with religion. However, courts in three more recent cases—*Brandon v. Board of Educ. of Guilderland,*[20] *Johnson v. Huntington Beach Union High School Dist.,*[21] and *Trietley v. Board of Educ. of the City of Buffalo*[22]—agreed that extracurricular prayer clubs violated the establishment clause. They reached identical conclusions through slightly different analyses under the three-part test. The *Brandon* and *Johnson* courts ruled that policies permitting the clubs would have the secular pur-

13. 421 F. Supp. 337 (D. Mass. 1976) (three-judge court).
14. 705 F.2d 1526 (11th Cir. 1983).
15. 557 F. Supp. 103 (D.N.M. 1983).

16. 548 F. Supp. 1161 (M.D. Tenn. 1982).
17. 387 Mass. 1201, 440 N.E.2d 1159 (1982).

18. 454 U.S. 263 (1981).
19. 237 F. Supp. 48 (W.D. Mich. 1965).
20. 635 F.2d 971 (2d Cir. 1980), *cert. denied,* 454 U.S. 1123 (1981).
21. 68 Cal. App. 3d 1, 137 Cal. Rptr. 43 (Cal. Ct. App. 1977), *cert. denied,* 434 U.S. 877 (1977).
22. 65 App. Div.2d 1, 409 N.Y.S.2d 912 (N.Y. App. Div. 1978).

pose of demonstrating a neutral school attitude toward extracurricular activities. On the other hand, the *Trietley* court focused on the activity of a prayer club, rather than on the school extracurricular policy that authorized the formation of the club, and decided that the club's purpose was religious.

The three courts agreed that the clubs would violate the second and third parts of the test. They found that the groups would, as their primary effect, advance the religious beliefs of their members. The courts also determined that the groups would require excessive entanglement of school officials with religion through teacher supervision for such purposes as ensuring safety and order, ensuring that activities during club meetings are voluntary, preventing discriminatory membership policies, and auditing club financial records.

In 1981 the Supreme Court muddied the constitutional waters by holding in *Widmar* that the First Amendment's guarantee of freedom of speech requires a public university in Missouri to allow students to form prayer clubs on campus. Though the university argued that the presence of prayer groups would violate the establishment clause, the Court ruled that allowing the clubs would pass the familiar three-part test. It first stated that opening a public university campus to prayer groups would serve a neutral, secular policy of maintaining the campus as an open forum for the exchange of ideas. The Court then held that any benefits to religion would be merely "incidental" consequences rather than primary effects of the clubs, because "an open forum in a public university does not confer any imprimatur of State approval on religious sects or practices"[23] and because any impact of such a club on a campus with over 100 recognized student groups would be minimal. Significantly, the Court noted with regard to the effect of university prayer groups, "University students are, of course, young adults. They are less impressionable than younger students and should be able to appreciate that the University's policy is one of neutrality toward religion."[24] Third, the Court found that excluding religious clubs from a public university campus would risk greater entanglement than admitting

them, because such an exclusion would mean that all extracurricular groups would have to be policed to ensure that they do not engage in religious activities. The Court also noted that college students often live on campus, with little chance of finding suitable places to worship off campus.

What is the impact of *Widmar* on the constitutionality of public school prayer clubs? At first glance, it might appear that *Widmar* overrules *Brandon, Johnson,* and *Trietley.* Indeed, in *Bender v. Williamsport*[25] a federal district court in Pennsylvania held that *Widmar* applies with equal force to public high school prayer clubs. That court ruled that students' freedom of speech under the First Amendment entitled them to meet for prayer, rejecting the school district's argument that allowing prayer groups to meet would violate the establishment clause. Using the three-part test, the court decided that (1) allowing the club to meet would serve the secular purpose of maintaining an open, neutral extracurricular policy; (2) high school students are mature enough not to interpret the school's acceptance of the club as tacit endorsement of the groups' religious doctrines and practices; and (3) teacher supervision would entail no more governmental entanglement with religion than a policeman's patrolling of a religious rally in a public park.

The United States Court of Appeals for the Fifth Circuit took the opposite tack, ruling in *Lubbock Civil Liberties Union v. Lubbock Independent School District*[26] that even after *Widmar*, prayer meetings in public schools violate the establishment clause. Also using the three-part test, the court decided first that the school district's policy authorizing prayer meetings was not merely a neutral policy granting equal, open access to extracurricular groups; rather, it was part of a comprehensive policy concerned with religious activities in school, and the school board's purpose in promulgating the policy was to promote religious meetings. The court then concluded that the policy's primary effect was to advance religion. It reasoned that allowing prayer meetings as part of an official extracurricular program would imply official ap-

proval of the meetings to impressionable elementary and secondary school children.[27] The court distinguished *Widmar* as applying to more mature college students. Finally, it ruled that the policy entailed excessive governmental entanglement with religion through the teacher supervision required to protect school property and ensure that the activities of prayer clubs were voluntary.

As the conflicting *Bender* and *Lubbock* decisions demonstrate, *Widmar* leaves the law about extracurricular prayer clubs in public schools unclear. Some of the comments in the *Widmar* opinion suggest that the Supreme Court would strike down prayer clubs below the college level. The Court's observations in *Widmar* that college students are less impressionable than younger students and that college students living on campus often have no suitable off-campus alternative for group prayer suggest that it would distinguish between colleges and public schools. In addition, the Court denied certiorari in both *Brandon* and *Lubbock* after its decision in *Widmar*, allowing those decisions to stand on the heels of *Widmar*. In short, it is probable, though hardly certain at this time, that extracurricular prayer clubs in public schools violate the establishment clause.

Try a factual twist on the prayer club cases: Would it be constitutional to allow students to meet in prayer groups that are independent of a school's official extracurricular program? For example, could students form a prayer group that met at the school during evening, nonschool hours? The answer, perhaps surprisingly, probably is yes. Courts around the country have upheld policies permitting religious congregations to use school facilities for worship during nonschool hours on the same basis as nonreligious groups. In *Country Hills Christian Church v. Unified School District No. 512,*

23. 454 U.S. at 274.
24. *Id.,* n. 14.

25. No. 82-0692 (M.D. Pa., filed May 12, 1983).
26. 669 F.2d 1038 (5th Cir. 1982), *cert. denied.* 103 S. Ct. 800 (1983).

27. A distinction based on the age of the audience is familiar in establishment clause analysis. For example, although officially sanctioned audible prayer at the start of a school day is unconstitutional, courts have ruled that legislatures and public governing boards may begin their sessions with prayer. *See, e.g.,* Marsh v. Chambers, 51 U.S.L.W. 5162 (1983); Bogen v. Doty, 598 F.2d 1110 (8th Cir. 1979); Voswinkel v. City of Charlotte, 495 F. Supp. 588, 597 (W.D.N.C. 1980); Colo v. Treasurer and Receiver General, 398 Mass. 550, 392 N.E.2d 1195 (1979); Lincoln v. Page, 109 N.H. 30, 241 A.2d 799 (1968).

Shawnee Mission, Kansas[28] and *Resnick v. East Brunswick Township Board of Educ.*,[29] those courts have ruled that such policies have the secular purpose of maintaining school facilities as open forums for community activities during nonschool hours,[30] that activities under such policies are sufficiently divorced from the official activities during the school day to avoid the implication of official school support, and that such open-door policies require no entangling supervision. Accordingly, students who may not meet in official extracurricular prayer groups during the school day nevertheless should be able to meet on school grounds for prayer if their groups meet wholly independently of the official school curricular and extracurricular program.

Graduation prayers

Question: May public schools conduct graduation ceremonies with prayers as invocations or benedictions?

Answer: Probably yes.

Discussion: Although prayer used as an invocation or benediction in public school graduation seems to resemble prayer used to start regular school days rather closely, courts have upheld graduation prayer. In *Grossberg v. Deusebio*[31] a federal district court upheld the use of prayer for an invocation at a Virginia high school graduation. Attendance at graduation was voluntary, and the senior class paid the expenses of the ceremony and decided whether to include an invocation in the program. The court acknowledged that an invocation is a religious act with the effect of advancing religion and that a graduation ceremony held on school grounds is an official public school event. But it distinguished graduation invocations in those cases from the prayers struck down in *Engel* and *Schempp* by noting that the forbidden prayers were part of the regular curricular program, supervised by teachers, with the purpose of supporting religious principles. In contrast, the court

stated, a graduation invocation is not a repetitive part of the year-long school program, and the overall graduation is a ceremonial rather than educational or religious activity. No state funding was required for this commencement exercise and the invocation lasted only a few minutes, posing "only a shadow of a danger" and causing no significant appearance of government support for religion.

In *Wood v. Mt. Lebanon Township School District*[32] and *Weist v. Mt. Lebanon School District*,[33] courts upheld the use of both invocation and benediction prayer in a graduation. In both cases, as in *Grossberg*, attendance at the graduation was voluntary. However, the school board adopted the program for the ceremony. Consistent with *Grossberg*, the courts explained that graduation prayer was not part of the formal daily curricular routine enforced through compulsory attendance and was at worst a harmless "technical infringement." The federal district court declared in *Wood* that the prayer had a secular purpose of permitting "customary remarks."

These cases appear to be inconsistent with the school prayer cases. Using the three-part test, it seems clear, first, that regardless of the secular, ceremonial purpose of a graduation as a whole, a prayer uttered during the ceremony undeniably has a religious purpose: to invoke divine blessing. Second, the primary effect of prayer during an official school function is to incorporate religious faith into the ceremony, thereby implying official support of religious doctrine and advancing religion. Third, prayer either selected or approved by school officials entails considerable government entanglement in religion. In addition, the voluntary nature of a graduation as a whole does not save one of its component activities from violating the establishment clause. Furthermore, it is incorrect under establishment clause analysis that a short graduation prayer is at worst a "technical infringement," posing "only a shadow of a danger." As the Supreme Court observed in *Schempp*, "it is no defense to urge that the religious practices here may be relatively minor encroachments on the First amendment. The breach of neutrality that is today a trickling stream may all

too soon become a raging torrent."[34] Despite the conflicts between cases that permit graduation prayer and cases that prohibit official prayer during the official school day, courts seem willing to give a tolerant constitutional wink at graduation prayer.[35]

A situation similar to prayer during graduations is prayer during school athletic events—for example, as an invocation or during half-time at high school football games. No published cases appear to have addressed this issue. In the spectrum between prohibited and permitted religious practices, such prayer seems to fall somewhere between graduation prayer and officially sanctioned prayer during the regular school day. Like graduation ceremonies, sporting events are separate from instruction and the school day, and attendance is voluntary. However, unlike graduations, athletic events are regularly recurring functions. Considered under the three-part test, prayer at athletic events has a religious purpose, it implies the school's approval of the religious message of the prayer, and it entangles school officials with religion through planning and approving the prayer.

Religious symbols

Question: May religious symbols be displayed in public school facilities?

Answer: Yes, if they are displayed to teach students about society's religious heritage rather than to show official support for religious beliefs.

Discussion: Just as the establishment clause prohibits officially sanctioned prayer as inappropriate public support for religious doctrine, so it prohibits the display of religious symbols in school to advance religious doctrine. The key questions are whether particular symbols are religious and whether they are displayed

---

28. No. 82-2345 (D. Kan. filed Mar. 29. 1983).

29. 77 N.J. 88, 389 A.2d 944 (1978).

30. For example. student religious groups in North Carolina could meet as part of a program under the Community Schools Act. N.C. GEN. STAT. § 115C-203 et seq., as long as admission to meetings is open to all members of the community.

31. 380 F. Supp. 285 (E.D. Va. 1974).

---

32. 342 F. Supp. 1293 (W.D. Pa. 1972).

33. 457 Pa. 166, 320 A.2d 362, cert. denied, 419 U.S. 967 (1974).

---

34. 374 U.S. at 225.

35. Courts have shown similar willingness to bend the establishment clause on other issues, such as invocations for legislative and public governing board sessions, the use of the motto "In God We Trust" on U.S. coins, and the reference to God in the pledge of allegiance. Aronow v. United States. 432 F.2d 242 (9th Cir. 1970); Voswinkel v. City of Charlotte. 495 F. Supp. 588; Colo v. Treasurer. 398 Mass. 550. Despite their religious content. such practices generally are upheld as secular—merely ceremonial and sapped of their devotional content over the course of history.

in a religious manner. In *Stone v. Graham*,[36] the United States Supreme Court addressed a Kentucky statute that required the posting of the Ten Commandments in classrooms. The Court struck the statute down under the establishment clause, explaining that the first four commandments (dealing with duties toward God) make the Ten Commandments a sacred text.

The court found that the statute had the purpose of inducing students to read, reflect on, and obey the Ten Commandments. It regarded as ineffective the following disclaimer required by the statute to appear on every copy of the Ten Commandments: "The secular application of the Ten Commandments is clearly seen in its adoption as the fundamental legal code of Western Civilization and the Common Law of the United States."

Determining whether a particular symbol is "religious" can be a vexing challenge for a school official. For example, in *Florey v. Sioux Falls Schools District 49-5*,[37] the United States Court of Appeals for the Eighth Circuit upheld a school board policy that permitted the use of religious symbols like crosses, menorahs, crescents, Stars of David, creches, and symbols of Native American religions "provided such symbols are displayed as an example of the cultural and religious heritage of the holiday and are temporary in nature." The court explained its decision within the framework of the three-part test. First, it said that the policy's secular purpose was to enhance students' knowledge of their religious and cultural heritage rather than to promote religious doctrine. It noted that the Supreme Court had commented in *Schempp* that the establishment clause does not prohibit the study of religion "when presented objectively as part of a secular program of education."[38] Second, the court concluded that school personnel in fact carried out the policy to achieve the primary effect of improving students' appreciation of their heritage rather than to spread religious doctrine. Third, it determined that the policy minimized government entanglement with religion by providing administrators and teachers with guidelines for deciding whether particular symbols are religious or secular.

Taken together, *Stone* and *Florey* are likely to cause confusion, controversy, and frustration for school officials and citizens in determining whether particular symbols are religious or secular. At the least, school districts that permit the display of religious symbols should be careful to anchor them conscientiously in a secular instructional context.

Holiday observances

Question: May a school observe religious holidays through activities involving music, art, literature, and drama?

Answer: Yes, if such activities are undertaken for the secular purpose of teaching students about society's religious heritage.

Discussion: In *Florey* the Eighth Circuit Court also addressed the constitutionality of the school district's policy permitting public schools to observe holidays "that have a religious and a secular basis," expressly including Christmas, Easter, Passover, Chanukah, St. Valentine's Day, St. Patrick's Day, Thanksgiving, and Halloween. Observances included the singing of Christmas carols. The court used the same three-part analysis it used to assess the constitutionality of the display of religious symbols and upheld the holiday observance rules.[39] It contrasted the secular goal of the policy with an example of an unconstitutional application of that policy: a Christmas quiz for kindergarten classes in which correct answers required students to acknowledge Jesus as their savior and to state that angels saluted his birth in song.

Bible distribution

Question: May school officials arrange or permit the distribution of Bibles to students on school grounds during the school day?

Answer: School officials may neither distribute Bibles to students nor authorize others to do so. It is not clear whether officials may permit others to leave Bibles

in a school for students to take as they please.

Discussion: Until 1978 courts around the nation unanimously vetoed the common practice of allowing representatives of groups like the Gideons to distribute Bibles to school children (*Tudor v. Board of Education*,[40] *Hernandez v. Hanson*,[41] *Goodwin v. Cross County School District*,[42] and *Brown v. Orange County Board of Public Instruction*[43]), holding that Bible distribution plainly serves the religious purpose of spreading Biblical doctrine to students, conveys the appearance of official support for these doctrines, and uses school facilities as the vehicle for distributing a religious text. This unanimity was broken in *Meltzer v. Board of Public Instruction of Orange County*.[44] In that case, the school district involved in *Brown v. Orange County* tinkered with its policy, permitting the local Gideons simply to leave Bibles on a table for students to take if they wished. The United States Court of Appeals for the Fifth Circuit upheld the new policy without explanation in an equally divided decision. Thorough scrutiny under the three-part test would suggest that the policy fails all three parts: it serves a religious purpose of facilitating the dissemination of religious doctrine; it might appear to put the official stamp of approval on that doctrine; and it permits the use of school facilities to spread that doctrine. Although *Meltzer* shows that at least one court has tolerated the "passive" approach to Bible distribution, it is hardly a decision on which school officials may confidently base a policy.

Conclusion

The Supreme Court's early opinions about devotional activities in public school in *Engel* and *Schempp* initially appeared clear and decisive. Regardless of public opinion about the wisdom of those decisions, at least they seemed to establish comprehensible guidelines about the question of school prayer. However, inconsistencies have developed in judicial

---

36. 449 U.S. 39 (1981).
37. 619 F.2d 1311 (8th Cir.). *cert. denied*, 449 U.S. 987 (1980).
38. 374 U.S. at 225.

39. The court sidestepped the question whether Christmas carols are religious in modern America. Instead, it observed that carols have assumed a cultural significance justifying their inclusion in public school education. The court reasoned that when an activity serves a primarily secular purpose, the inclusion of religious content does not make it unconstitutional.

40. 41 N.J. 31. 100 A.2d 857 (1953), *cert. denied* 348 U.S. 816 (1954).
41. 430 F. Supp. 1154 (D. Neb. 1977).
42. 394 F. Supp. 417 (E.D. Ark. 1973).
43. 128 So.2d 181 (Fla. Ct. App. 1960).
44. 577 F.2d 311 (5th Cir. 1978) (en banc) (per curiam). *cert. denied*, 439 U.S. 1089 (1979).

review of other school religious activities since those decisions. Courts in some cases strictly scrutinize practices to enforce the establishment clause vigorously. In other cases courts seem willing to permit considerable government accommodation of religious activity. The three-part test is helpful, but judicial manipulation of the test occasionally undermines its value.

Beyond the three-part test, a few analytic themes emerge from the cases discussed in this article. First, courts examine the purpose and implementation of activities. They sometimes have given passing constitutional grades to activities with religious content when they were instituted and executed in genuinely secular contexts (e.g., activities designed for historical, literary, or cultural instruction). They also address whether practices are religious or have been deemed by judicial fiat to be drained of their religious significance, transformed into traditional secular customs (e.g., graduation prayer and holiday observances). In addition, courts focus on the relation of religious activities to the regular school routine: activities connected to the regular school day generally have failed constitutional challenge (e.g., school prayer or extracurricular prayer clubs), while practices independent of the normal school day often have survived challenges (e.g., graduation prayer and prayer gatherings with no relation to the official curricular or extracurricular program). Finally, although the Supreme Court has plainly ruled that voluntariness is irrelevant to establishment clause analysis, some courts that have upheld religious activities nonetheless have cited the voluntary nature of those activities as significant factors in their decisions.

Judicial inconsistency is frustrating to school officials on the firing line who need clear guidelines to make sound decisions. Officials must work closely with their attorneys to heed judicial precedent when it is clear and to analyze issues under the general principles developed by the courts when no clear precedent lights the way. ●

The Fair Sentencing Act

(continued from page 16)

charging did not increase (despite the incentive the FSA supplies for multiple charging by not requiring written justification for consecutive sentences). Consecutive prison sentences did increase among those with multiple convictions, but the total number of charges did not have an increased effect on length of sentence after the FSA, and total length of sentence did not increase. Although the FSA did supply an opportunity to evade the FSA's provisions by determination of sentences in plea bargaining, this practice actually decreased significantly after the FSA. After the FSA, plea bargaining was more often formal (that is, recorded), but also fewer bargains involved sentence concessions. The FSA, by making sentences more predictable, may have encouraged some defendants to plead guilty without prosecutorial promises of lenient sentences.

Suspension of sentences and imposition of CYO status were two other ways of getting around the FSA's provisions; however, CYO commitments did not increase in frequency after the FSA, and suspension of sentences actually became less frequent. Contrary to the expectations of some, trial court arrest-to-disposition time did not increase after the FSA; in fact, it decreased, probably because jury trials (which are very time-consuming) became even rarer after the FSA than formerly and dismissals increased slightly. Also, sentencing procedure under the FSA generally did not become as onerous as some critics had feared; the frequent use of presumptive sentences and the persistence of sentence bargaining (though at a reduced rate) obviated judicial findings for most felony sentences.

The FSA apparently is not adding to the increase in the prison population, despite fears that it would. Although the probability of active imprisonment increased after the FSA, the length of time to be served in prison generally was reduced by the fact that most active sentences were grouped around the presumptive level. The net effect of the FSA may actually be to reduce the prison population slightly compared with the level it would reach by 1986.

The picture of the FSA that emerges from the Institute's study is that felony sentencing has become more predictable and perhaps even fairer (in the sense of lessened racial disparity). Furthermore, there have apparently been no widespread efforts to undermine the legislation by administrative tactics and no deleterious consequences for trial court efficiency and the prison population.

The study's results should be interpreted cautiously. They concern only the first year of operation of the FSA, and criminal justice officials' response to the legislation may change. But for the present, it is fair to conclude that the FSA has brought change in the direction desired by its proponents ●

Recent Publications of the
Institute of Government

North Carolina Legislation 1983: A Summary of Legislation in the 1983 General Assembly of Interest to North Carolina Public Officials. Edited by Ann L. Sawyer. 1983. $10.00.

This comprehensive summary of the General Assembly's enactments during the 1983 legislative session is written by Institute faculty members who are experts in the respective fields touched by the new statutes.

The Safe Roads Act of 1983. A Summary and Compilation of Statutes Amended or Affected by the Act. Compiled by James C. Drennan. 1983. $5.00.

This publication summarizes North Carolina's new laws that pertain to drunken driving. It includes an appendix with the latest revisions of the statutes affected by the Safe Roads Act.

An Introduction to Municipal Zoning. Revised edition. By Philip P. Green, Jr. 1983. $4.50.

This new edition is designed as background reading for all zoning board members and others involved in local zoning.

Form of Government of North Carolina Cities. 1983 edition. Compiled by David M. Lawrence. $4.50.

This booklet sets out the form and structure of the governing board for each North Carolina city and town with a population in 1983 of 500 or more. It also specifies whether the municipality operates under the manager plan or the mayor-council plan and includes summary statistics for various population categories of cities and towns.

Index of Computer Hardware and Software in Use in North Carolina Local Governments. 1983. $6.00.

This publication contains information about the types of computer equipment, applications, software, and data processing arrangements that are used by local governments across North Carolina.

County Salaries in North Carolina. Compiled by Elizabeth Pace and Peggy Merris. 1983. $6.00.

This annual study, published since 1950, contains information on current salaries and personnel practices in all North Carolina counties. All major county positions are included as well as those of some assistants and deputies and other positions in which county officials have expressed interest.

Orders and inquiries should be sent to the Publications Office, Institute of Government, Knapp Building 059A, The University of North Carolina at Chapel Hill, Chapel Hill, N.C. 27514. Please enclose a check or purchase order for the amount of the order, plus 3 per cent sales tax (4 per cent in Orange County). A complete publications catalog is available from the Publications Office upon request.

CPSIA information can be obtained
at www.ICGtesting.com
Printed in the USA
BVHW050030061118
532207BV00022B/2857/P